About This Book

Why Is This Topic Important?

The use of psychological tests for selection and development has been increasing rapidly over the past two decades, particularly as the Internet has become such a popular vehicle for such testing. Most users of these tests, however, have been individuals with little or no training in their use and the various issues inherent in this use. Because the many available texts on testing typically are theoretical in their approach and aimed at audiences of students or professional psychologists, we saw a need for a how-to-do-it book aimed at test users—HR professionals, trainers, line managers, and others who use tests regularly in their work. This book is the result.

What Can You Achieve with This Book?

Our book provides an easily understood, practical approach to using individual assessments to improve both selecting of new employees and planning training and development throughout the employee life cycle, including mentoring, out-placement, and team building. The rationale underlying individual assessment—improving the match between the person and job—is clearly spelled out, together with the various issues and pitfalls that may be encountered during this process.

How Is This Book Organized?

The book is divided into six chapters that take the reader sequentially through the individual assessment process, highlighting the procedures that need to be followed at each step. Case examples illustrate most of the steps involved, and the appendices provide models of competency and samples of individual assessment reports at three levels—entry, supervisor/first-line manager, and senior manager/executive.

About Pfeiffer

Pfeiffer serves the professional development and hands-on resource needs of training and human resource practitioners and gives them products to do their jobs better. We deliver proven ideas and solutions from experts in HR development and HR management, and we offer effective and customizable tools to improve workplace performance. From novice to seasoned professional, Pfeiffer is the source you can trust to make yourself and your organization more successful.

Essential Knowledge Pfeiffer produces insightful, practical, and comprehensive materials on topics that matter the most to training and HR professionals. Our Essential Knowledge resources translate the expertise of seasoned professionals into practical, how-to guidance on critical workplace issues and problems. These resources are supported by case studies, worksheets, and job aids and are frequently supplemented with CD-ROMs, websites, and other means of making the content easier to read, understand, and use.

Essential Tools Pfeiffer's Essential Tools resources save time and expense by offering proven, ready-to-use materials—including exercises, activities, games, instruments, and assessments—for use during a training or team-learning event. These resources are frequently offered in looseleaf or CD-ROM format to facilitate copying and customization of the material.

Pfeiffer also recognizes the remarkable power of new technologies in expanding the reach and effectiveness of training. While e-hype has often created whizbang solutions in search of a problem, we are dedicated to bringing convenience and enhancements to proven training solutions. All our e-tools comply with rigorous functionality standards. The most appropriate technology wrapped around essential content yields the perfect solution for today's on-the-go trainers and human resource professionals.

www.pfeiffer.com

Essential resources for training and HR professionals

For Jeanette and Delores
For their support and affection
and for putting up with us.

Using Individual Assessments in the Workplace

A Practical Guide for HR Professionals, Trainers, and Managers

Leonard D. Goodstein, Ph.D.
Erich P. Prien, Ph.D.

Pfeiffer
A Wiley Imprint
www.pfeiffer.com

Published by Pfeiffer
An Imprint of Wiley
989 Market Street, San Francisco, CA 94103-1741
www.pfeiffer.com

For additional copies/bulk purchases of this book in the U.S. please contact 800-274-4434.

Pfeiffer books and products are available through most bookstores. To contact Pfeiffer directly call our Customer Care Department within the U.S. at 800-274-4434, outside the U.S. at 317-572-3985, fax 317-572-4002, or visit www.pfeiffer.com.

Pfeiffer also publishes its books in a variety of electronic formats. Some content that appears in print may not be available in electronic books.

Library of Congress Cataloging-in-Publication Data

Goodstein, Leonard David.
  Using individual assessments in the workplace : a practical guide for HR professionals, trainers, and managers / Leonard D. Goodstein, Erich P. Prien.
     p. cm.
  Includes bibliographical references and index.
  ISBN-13: 978-0-7879-8256-0 (cloth)
  ISBN-10: 0-7879-8256-3 (cloth)
  1. Personnel management—Psychological aspects. 2. Psychological tests. 3. Psychology, Industrial. I. Prien, Erich P., 1928- II. Title.
  HF5549.G6517 2006
  658.3001'9—dc22
                                        2006004173

Acquiring Editor: Matthew Davis   Production Editor: Dawn Kilgore
Director of Development: Kathleen Dolan Davies   Editor: Rebecca Taff
Developmental Editor: Susan Rachmeler   Manufacturing Supervisor: Becky Carreño

Printed in the United States of America

Printing   10 9 8 7 6 5 4 3 2 1

Contents

Foreword

In 1964 I was one year beyond my doctorate—don't bother with the math; I assure you it was a long time ago—and as the authors, Goodstein and Prien, describe it, a "newly minted Ph.D." Goodstein and Prien use that phrase in the context of potential users of this book. Having their book back then would have saved me considerable angst and labor. That year, my second one as an assistant professor of psychology at the University of Richmond, I joined a local consulting firm on a part-time basis both to learn and to earn some extra income. As I recall, my academic salary at the time was about $9,000 per academic year. Some extra money meant a lot. The firm was founded and run by an industrial-organizational psychologist originally educated at Purdue—in other words, well-trained in psychological testing. We psychologists in his firm were involved in providing reports for client businesses in the Richmond area so they could decide whether to hire or promote someone. The reports that we dictated into a Dictaphone and that a secretary then typed (dated technology to be sure) were based on (a) results from a battery of psychological tests, including many still in use today such as the Wonderlic (IQ), Guilford-Zimmerman (personality), and Watson-Glaser (critical thinking); (b) an individual interview with the candidate; and (c) our own observations.

Practically from the moment I joined the firm, I was thrown into the deep end of the pool and largely had to swim on my own. Yes, I had some guidance from the boss, but not much, and my fellow psychologists taught me a few tricks of the trade, yet for all practical purposes I was swimming without fins, much less a life jacket. This book could have been my life jacket. While I didn't drown, I had to tread water for too long a period of time and felt from time to time as if I had lead feet and was sinking. Had I been able to learn from Goodstein and Prien, two of the most seasoned, experienced, and competent psychologists in the field of psychological testing today, I could have saved considerable time and stayed in the deep end of the pool all day with no fear of drowning.

A significant problem today is that too many people, most of whom not being psychologists, are using psychological tests and do not know how to swim. This life-saving book in the world of psychological testing is one of a kind—the only primer I know of that explains in clear language not only how to use tests but how to assess whether the assessment instrument itself is worth using.

One reason that so many people, whether qualified or not, are using psychological tests today is that we have learned over the years—the hard way—the economic consequences of poor selection and placement decisions. Companies pay an enormous price, both economically and psychologically, for hiring the wrong people, for placing them in the wrong jobs, and for training them to do the jobs they were not qualified for in the first place.

While I am a great supporter of and believer in spending resources on training and development, far more important, in my judgment, is spending resources on selection and placement. Getting the right person in the right job takes care of most motivational issues, and in turn, has a considerably positive impact on performance. I have often said to managers, "You can hardly spend too much time on selection and placement decisions." Getting these decisions right takes us a long way down the road to organizational effectiveness and high performance. My point is that proper utilization of the lessons and experience conveyed in this book will contribute to the bottom line.

My early days of learning psychological assessment and how to apply these results to important decisions have been important to advancing my career and effectiveness as a consultant. I have used the learning not only for selection and placement purposes, but for helping people with (a) career decisions; (b) professional development, for example, whether to pursue management and leadership or stay with an individual contributor track; and (c) their role within a group that aspires to be a team. In other words, due to my assessment experience, I think I am a better coach for managers, leaders, and professionals in general than I otherwise would be. If I had had this Goodstein and Prien primer in my briefcase at the outset, how much better might I have turned out? Perhaps not much better, after all, I do have my genetic limitations. But I would have learned faster and made fewer mistakes—even in the deep end of the pool.

W. Warner Burke
Edward Lee Thorndike Professor of
Psychology and Education
Teachers College, Columbia University

Foreword

This is an important, accessible, timely book written by two eminently qualified psychologists. It is the product of two distinguished scientist/practitioners with wide-ranging and complementary experience in the worlds of personality and industrial/organisational psychology. To have an appreciation of the two different worlds of business and academia is unusual but critically important in order to write such a book as this. To be both a researcher and a practitioner can bring a benefit to any author, and this practical, sensible, well-informed book attests to the breadth of both authors.

This is essentially a practical book. It is a primer for the practitioner interested in the area of individual differences. But it is informed with state-of-the-art theory. It was the famous psychologist, Kurt Lewin, who said, "There is nothing as practical as good theory."

Many people must get involved in the business of assessment. This occurs in recruitment and selection, in appraisal and development, and in out-placement counseling and awareness training. This book will provide those involved in such procedures the understanding and the tools to do a better job in each of these areas.

People are complex and capricious. And in most businesses these two characteristics can be both their most important asset but also their greatest liability. It is critical to be able to assess the impact of these characteristics as they play out in the workplace.

We have known for nearly one hundred years that the best employee is about 2.5 times more productive than the worst employee. Good workers can act as models for others; while bad workers can sour and poison a workplace. Managers need to know how to accurately assess and understand their colleagues and their reports. This book will be an invaluable aid to the hard-working manager trying to ensure he or she has the best workers and gets the most out of them.

More and more we are seeing the emergence of coaching as a tool for improving job performance. Many practitioners want to have an economic, valid, and sensitive method to assess others for a wide variety of purposes. This book gives them precisely that.

Most people in business are in the business of assessment. And most are not trained in how to do it well. They don't know the range of tools available or how to select the best one. They need advice on best practices and processes. Managers need to know *what* to assess and *how* to do it. They need to know where to get advice, and equally what to do with their assessments once they have obtained them. And this is where this extremely useful and straightforward book fits in.

Assessment is too important to leave open to amateurs. This book is written for busy practitioners—and not only those in human resources. This book purports to be both a primer and a manual. But it is more than that. It is also a guide and a tool kit. Clearly written, well-informed and eminently practical, it is sure to be a hit with all busy professionals in the business of assessment.

Adrian Furnham
Professor of Psychology
University College, London

Chapter One

Introduction

Over the past decade, the use of psychological testing for employee selection, training and development, and out-placement has greatly increased, which has produced a need for greater understanding of testing and its use in conducting individual assessments for employment-related purposes. To the best of our knowledge, there is no readable, readily understandable, yet comprehensive introductory book on this important management tool.

For Whom Did We Write This Book?

In writing this book, we had at least four audiences in mind: first, managers who routinely use individual assessments in helping them make human resources decisions; second, human resources professionals who actually conduct such assessments, often without an adequate understanding of the inherent issues involved in their work; third, trainers who often include tests and other instruments as part of a training exercise; and, fourth, those others who are interested in how individual assessments should be conducted, especially those persons who have been the targets of such a process.

We would expect that managers reading this book would have a better understanding of what to expect from a competent individual assessment and be better able to contract for such services. For the human resources professionals, we hope that reading this book would lead to an increase in their assessment skills and an improvement in the quality of their assessment reports. We believe that trainers would improve their use of instruments in their presentations. Finally, we would expect that the general public interested in these matters would acquire a better understanding of the individual assessment process, of how that process improves human resources decisions in the workplace, as well as its limitations and what to expect as the subject of such a process.

While professional psychologists are not one of our primary audiences, we do think that they may find this book useful. Newly minted psychologists without much practical, hands-on experience will find this volume useful in filling in some gaps in their knowledge and skills base. Others may find it useful in helping their clients or prospective clients in better understanding what they do. We look forward to hearing from them and others about the usefulness of this product.

Of course, there are many books on psychological testing available. Just check out the website of any bookseller. Indeed, we have written several of them. But they fall into two major categories: the books intended for college- or graduate-level courses in testing and assessment and those that are essentially arguments against their use for a variety of reasons. As the readers of this volume will learn, improvements in the technology underlying testing has improved over the past two decades, and these arguments have lost their cogency.

What Are Our Recommendations?

Much of this book is prescriptive, urging the adoption of a variety of techniques and procedures that we believe will improve the quality of the individual assessment process. But we also recognize that it is extremely unlikely that all of them will be enthusiastically adopted by practitioners. Rather, we hope that readers will sort out those recommendations that fit their approach to assessment and that they believe will enhance their effectiveness. To the extent that this occurs, we will regard our time in writing this to have been well spent.

How Is This Book Organized?

Chapter Two: The Practice of Individual Assessment

The practice of individual assessment covers a broad spectrum from administering a single test to an individual for a specific purpose to administering and interpreting a comprehensive battery of tests to evaluate an individual in order to understand that person in some depth. The purpose of this guide is, through the use of a five-step model, to lead practitioners of assessment through the necessary steps of the individual assessment process across this spectrum. This is a what, how, and why manual that aims to prepare or enhance the level of understanding and skills that assessors need at three levels to perform this job competently. The focus of this book is on assessment in the workplace for selection, evaluation, coaching, and training and development. Finally, the impact of information technology and the Internet on individual assessment is reviewed.

Chapter Three: Psychological Measurement

Psychological testing and the statistics used to understand testing depend on the assumptions involved in the normal distribution curve. Any test used in assessment must be supported by evidence of some form of reliability and validity, ensuring that the test scores provide trustworthy information. Further, normative data, which provide the essential framework for understanding this information, also must be available, usually in the test manual; that is, test scores cannot exist in a vacuum. The available psychological tests fit into four major categories: personal/interpersonal functioning, specific job competencies, general intellectual functioning, and miscellaneous. There is strong evidence for the validity of most of these, as well as for the behavioral interview.

Chapter Four: Collecting and Analyzing Assessment Data

The process of individual assessment requires the collection and integration of data about individuals on the one hand and jobs on the other hand. These data are the raw ingredients for the assessment process and require a skilled assessor to extract the meaning from the raw data. In this sense, the assessor becomes the processor of the data.

The implementation of our five-step model for conducting this process is provided as a guide to both the collection and analysis of the assessment data, together with a discussion of some critical issues such as choosing assessment measures, learning about new tests, and benchmarking.

Chapter Five: Developing and Integrating Individual Assessment Data

A number of sources of information can be included in an individual assessment. They include the resume; interview; psychological testing, including measures of personality, specific job competencies, cognitive ability, management and leadership skills, and honesty/integrity; work products; job samples; and observed behavior. Choosing among these measures is always a function of the requirements of the job under scrutiny. These data then need to be analyzed, inferences drawn from them, values placed on the inferences, and, finally, conclusions need to be drawn.

Chapter Six: Reporting Individual Assessment Results

Preparing a final report on an assessment requires an in-depth understanding of the individual in relation to the requirements of a specific job. Such reports require synthesizing a vast amount of information. A format for such reports is provided comprising four parts: (1) Identifying Information; (2) Functional Analysis; (3) Person/Job Fit; and (4) Conclusions and Recommendations. The recurrent need is to communicate effectively to the end user of the report. This format provides an approach that meets that need. A series of forty questions that serve as a quality-control mechanism is also provided. The use of individual assessment reports for planning training and development through the employee lifecycle, including mentoring, outplacement, and team building, is highlighted. There is a need for future-oriented job analysis to enhance the value of individual assessment reports.

Appendices

There are nine appendices, the first of which contains a list of recommended readings that will further extend the readers' understanding of this important area. Following an appendix with a sample position description, there is a brief discussion of how to conduct a job analysis. The next two appendices provide samples of the competency specifications for first-line supervisors and then managers/executives to complement those for entry-level jobs found in Chapter Two. These are followed by three appendices, each containing a sample individual assessment report—one each for entry-level, first-line supervisor, and manager/executive positions, respectively. The final appendix contains a selective listing of the various psychological tests that we have found useful in our practice, including information about their publishers.

In writing this book we have continuously been aware of the prevailing problems, issues, and standards of our profession, especially those related to psychological testing and individual assessment. Readers are also urged to become acquainted with the three standard-setting references on psychological testing and individual assessment: (1) the *Standards for Educational and Psychological Testing*, established by a joint task force of the American Educational Research Association, American Psychological Association, and National Council on Measurement in Education (1999); (2) *Uniform Guidelines on Employee Selection Procedures* (1978), promulgated jointly by the U.S. Equal Opportunities Commission and the Departments of Justice and Labor; and (3) *Principles for the Validation and Use of Personnel Selection Procedures* (4th ed.), established by the Society for Industrial and Organizational Psychology (2003). These three references set the criteria by which psychological tests and individual assessment processes are evaluated and have been the bedrock on which we have based our many years of practice and this book.

Both of us have spent the major portion of our professional work focused on the development and use of psychological tests. Between the two of us, there is almost a century of professional work in testing, including decades of experience in conducting countless individual assessments. We hope that we have been able to use that knowledge and experience to provide readers with an understandable, yet solid knowledge of the individual assessment process and how tests are used in that process.

Chapter Two

The Practice of Individual Assessment

When you finish reading this book, you should have a basic understanding of the individual assessment process and procedures and its application in the management of human resources, including selection, promotion, training and development, and out-placement. While the goals of each of these human resources functions is somewhat different, the role of individual assessment is the same in each—to develop as complete a picture as possible of an individual, not only to help maximize his or her potential contribution to the organization but also to assist that person as an individual in self-understanding and his or her career path. For our purposes we will separate selection on the one hand from promotion, training and development, and out-placement on the other hand, as the former focuses on the organization and its needs, while the latter three all involve more of a focus on the individual and his or her needs.

The level of importance and complexity of the job should establish the necessary degree of clarity and completeness of the picture required. More senior jobs, ones with considerable independent decision-making authority, expose the organization to greater risk than those on the factory or sales floor, thus requiring a more complete picture, a much sharper one. Given those risks, we need to more fully understand both the requirements of any particular job and the strengths and weaknesses of this particular person to meet those requirements. Thus as we move to fill more senior positions in the organizational hierarchy, the number and importance of the necessary competencies grows, as does the importance of the person-job fit. Understanding the two basic elements inherent in every individual assessment—the job and its requirements on the one hand and the individual with strengths and weaknesses on the other—is a recurrent theme throughout this book.

Another focus of this book is to provide information on assessing and qualifying potential providers of assessment services when you contract for individual assessment services and to help you to determine the skill level and general competence of those who are offering to do assessments. Unfortunately, the practice of individual assessment is weakly regulated and there are far too many unqualified practitioners, as well as many who practice well beyond their skills and qualifications. Such performers can only be identified by educating consumers to understand the nature of quality assessment services and to insist on receiving such quality. Later in this chapter and in the sample reports contained in Appendices F, G, and H, we provide criteria by which the educated consumer can evaluate the quality of the work he or she is receiving.

What Is Individual Assessment?

In broadest terms, individual assessment is the process of (a) collecting information about a person in order to evaluate him or her, typically against the requirements of a specific job; (b) then analyzing and interpreting that information in order to make inferences about that person's future job performance; and (c) making recommendations about that individual—should this person be hired, promoted, offered training and development opportunities, or provided coaching and/or mentoring. We shall return to this increasingly important issue of using individual assessment to evaluate the specific developmental needs of an individual in Chapter Six.

What Does an Assessor Need to Know?

The practice of individual assessment requires that assessors themselves have certain competencies. However, the types and level of the required competencies vary, depending on the type of assessment to be conducted. As we continue through the levels of assessment, from the simplest to the most complex, it should become apparent that a progression of assessor competencies is required, ranging from the application of basic and fairly straightforward operations at the entry-level activity up to the higher, more complex levels of assessment expertise. Generally, the more complex operations or activities the assessor expects to encounter, the greater will be the need for education, training, and experience. For our purposes we are categorizing this continuum of competencies into three broad, sometimes overlapping levels of knowledge, skills, and abilities (KSAs) (Primoff, 1957). In discussing these three levels of necessary KSAs it will become clear that, as the complexity of competency requirements increases, the education and experience requirements also increase (McClelland, 1973). But, in general, there are opportunities at all three levels to work competently in individual assessment.

The Three Levels of Assessor Competencies

Level 1. The basic entry-level assignment (Level 1), typically with job titles such as human resources (HR) associate, requires basic common sense as well as the ability to follow strictly the printed instructions for test administration, plus a willingness to maintain the confidentiality of the test files and to execute standard office procedures. The specific tasks at this level begin with a careful reading of the test administration instructions before actually administering any test to examinees, carefully timing and proctoring tests, and ensuring that examinees understand and follow test instructions.

This level of competence ordinarily requires an undergraduate degree in psychology, sociology, human resources management, or the equivalent. An associate of arts degree with some years of relevant experience is often seen as a substitute for a bachelor's degree. Occasionally, individuals without any collegiate degree who have years of experience in an organization are promoted to these positions.

The specific knowledge, skills, and abilities required for Level 1 practitioners to process a variety of common entry-level standardized jobs include:

- Competence to conduct standardized job analyses, including identification of the job content or work activities and the required job competencies.
- Ability to write content- or behaviorally oriented job analysis procedures in relation to their intended use.
- Knowledge of the techniques used to assess individuals' job-related competencies.
- Competence to perform individual assessments for various purposes, including administration and scoring of standardized tests, collecting and recording of performance observations, and evaluation of data obtained.
- Understanding of basic business operations and practices and the implications for human resources management.
- Knowledge and understanding of ethical and professional standards in conducting individual assessment.

All that is required at this beginning level is the desire and willingness to acquire the necessary skills by reading, study, and mentorship.

From this entry-level HR associate position, additional experience and in-service education and training can lead to promotion to senior HR associate, at which time one would perform a greater variety of specific, professional-level tasks, tasks that require a more in-depth understanding of the principles of psychological measurement and individual assessment.

At this somewhat more advanced level, the senior HR associate can perform a variety of assessment tasks, including some basic organization and integration of data for the final report, as well as making some basic decisions about how to manage the assessment data. To perform these tasks, the senior HR associate needs to possess additional knowledge and skills, those that would be gained through experience on the job as well as through on-the-job training. In addition, the individual needs a reasonable level of curiosity and the basic initiative needed to participate and function in a real-world setting.

Level 2. The second level of assessment practice involves a reasonably broad knowledge of the theory underlying psychological testing and measurement; experience with the administration, scoring, and interpretation of the most widely used measures of individual performance; skill in conducting and using job analyses; and an ability to integrate the results of the psychological tests with the job requirements identified in the job analysis. Further, this second-level practitioner needs to understand the culture of the organization within which he or she works and the unique demands that this culture places on individuals at work. Last and certainly not unimportant, those professionals working at this level need to be able to maintain confidentiality about both the tests that they use and the results produced by those who take these tests.

The level of competence required for conducting independent, individual assessment in a small organization at Level 2 ordinarily requires a master's degree in industrial/organizational (I/O) psychology, human resources management, or some related field. Persons trained in a related field will profit from participating in half- or full-day workshops sponsored by professional associations (such as the Society for Human Resources Management or American Society for Training and Development).

The second-level practitioner competencies include all those of the Level 1 practitioners plus the following:

- Competence to conduct job analyses of complex and specialized jobs, including managerial jobs.
- Knowledge of psychometric principles and practices for the construction, standardization, use, and evaluation of measurement of individual differences, as well as knowledge of the current research.

- Competence to judge and evaluate the usefulness of criterion measures.
- Knowledge of the factors involved in or contributing to adverse impact of a personnel decision-making procedure.
- Knowledge of occupation-related education and training practices, resources, and individual options for acquiring necessary skills and qualifications.
- Knowledge of the principles of human learning as related to individual and group formal training and on-the-job training.
- Knowledge of the impact of experiential learning and coaching on human performance at work.
- Knowledge of group dynamics that explain individual and group behavior and provide the rationale for constructive actions.
- Knowledge of the sources of individual, group, and organizational performance/effectiveness criteria.
- Identification of the demands placed upon incumbents by the organizational culture and the specific work setting.
- Competence to perform individual assessments for a variety of jobs, including managerial jobs, by using both standardized tests and more informal procedures.
- Understanding of the organization, its strategy, its culture, and its operations and their implications for human resources management.
- Knowledge, understanding, and adherence to the standards of professional, ethical, and legal standards in conducting individual assessments.

Level 3. The highest level of competence, Level 3, involves (a) an in-depth knowledge of measurement theory and practice, including advanced statistical procedures; (b) an advanced understanding of the broad range of the available psychological tests and how to evaluate their usefulness; (c) knowledge of and skills in conducting job analyses of complex, senior-level jobs and skills in and comfort with assessing executive-level individuals; (d) an ability to integrate and synthesize the results of the individual assessment with those of the job analysis; (e) the knowledge and skill to conduct organization-based reliability and validation studies; and (f) the skills to supervise others in aspects of each of these tasks, as required.

Practitioners at this level ordinarily hold a terminal professional degree, that is, a doctorate in I/O psychology or a related discipline and would have had considerable supervised experience in each of these areas as part of their education and training. Such individuals would routinely participate in professional organization activities, and those in independent practice would be expected to hold a current state license as a psychologist.

The third-level practitioner competencies include all those included in the two lower levels plus the following:

- Competence to conduct job analyses of highly complex jobs, including executive jobs.

- Knowledge of the characteristics, strengths and weaknesses, and methodologies of scaling techniques used in human measurement.

- Ability to analyze and evaluate technical problems/issues within the context of legal requirements and regulations.

- Ability to organize/coordinate research to establish validity of assessment processes.

- Knowledge of factors in research settings that affect research operations and results.

- Competence in analyzing the organizational culture as well as specific work settings and their implications for human resources management.

- Competence to perform individual assessments for a wide variety of jobs, including executive-level jobs, by using both standardized tests and more informal procedures.

- Ability to write a cogent, informative report on an individual assessment.
- Ability to identify and practice the specific behaviors of an assessor as established by professional/ethical standards.
- Ability to analyze and evaluate the actions and activities of oneself and others in relation to the principles and standards of professional ethics.
- Knowledge of and adherence to professional standards applicable to the practice of professional human resource management.
- Competence to conduct independently a variety of research studies, including those evaluating the reliability and validity of various tests and other procedures in an organization.
- Capacity to function independently and to supervise others in performing individual assessments and related tasks.
- Ability to provide helpful feedback to persons based on an individual assessment
- Ability to facilitate decision making by end users based on assessment data.
- Ability to use the principles and techniques of employee counseling, coaching, and mentoring for effective performance (Prien & Macey, 1984.)

An Additional Consideration

Overall, the philosophy and strategy we advocate for the individual assessment practitioner is to learn as much as one can about individual assessment. Further, we strongly believe that it is also important to be clear what you do not understand or know, and once you have identified any gaps in your knowledge, work diligently to close them. The practice of individual assessment is an ever-expanding one, and continual exposure to education and training materials is necessary to maintain competence. For example, the entry-level practitioner needs to identify and fill the gaps in his or her knowledge while seeking and securing mentoring from a more senior professional. The doctoral-level practitioner is expected to subscribe to and read professional journals and regularly attend professional conferences (Schippmann, Hawthorne, & Schmidt, 1992). There is an abundance of material available at every level, and some especially pertinent sources are included in the list of recommended reading (Appendix A) and the References.

The Individual Assessment Model

The individual assessment process that is described in this guide is not based on any theoretical model, but rather is a description of the actual assessment process, step-by-step, as it occurs typically in real-world settings, especially in those organizations that adhere to the highest level of professional competence and ethicality (Prien, Schippmann, & Prien, 2003). We will present the outline of this model here initially as part of our introduction to the individual assessment process, and then return to it in Chapter Four, where we will explain how it can and should be applied.

This process can best be understood as involving five steps, as presented in Figure 2.1 on the next page.

Organization and Work Setting

The first step in the model involves developing an understanding of the organizational and work setting in which this specific job will be performed. In following our model of individual assessment, it is important to understand that all jobs with the same title are *not* created equal; therefore, the focus must be on the specific work situation and the business environment in which it operates. For example, jobs with the same job title may be very different in terms of the pressure for performance or for quality, or for problems faced in dealing with an especially difficult supervisor or a work group inhospitable to a newcomer. Failure to build understanding of such

Figure 2.1. Model of the Individual Assessment Process

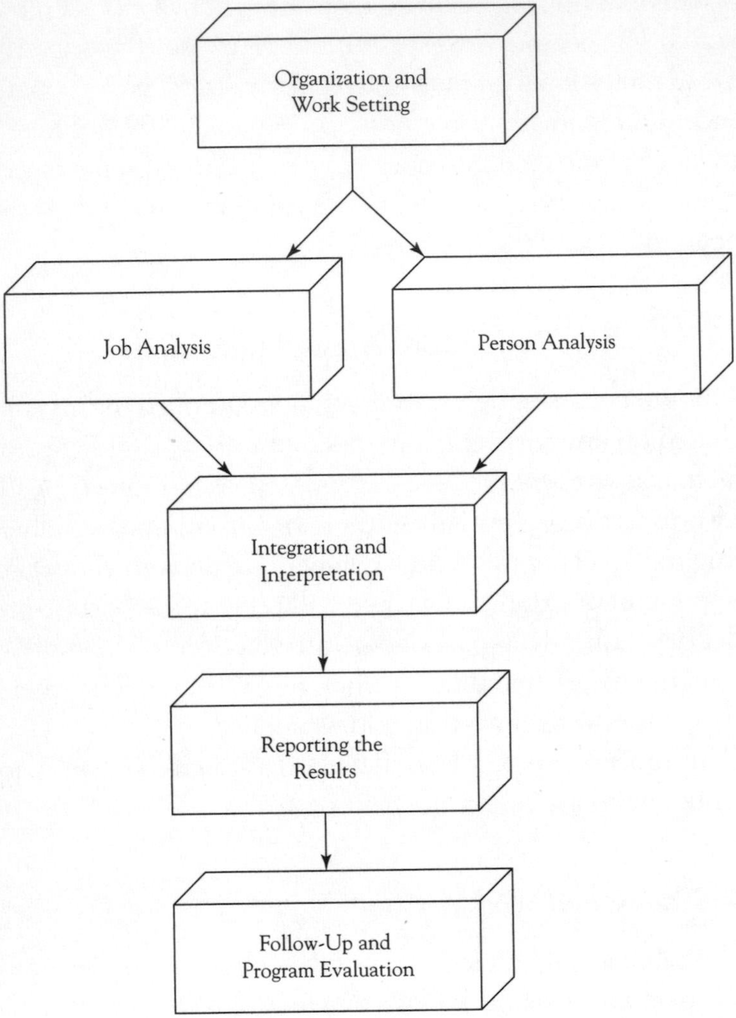

factors into the assessment process inevitably will diminish the quality and usefulness of the final product of the assessment.

In the practice of individual assessment, the client's business operations—its business strategies, plans, and problems—are of singular importance in designing and carrying out the assessment process. Furthermore, those issues should also have an impact on the inferences and conclusions drawn from the raw data and on the final report (Matarazzo, 1990). Thus each assessment demands that as much as possible be known about the organization, its culture, how it functions, and the environment in which it operates. Obviously, the overall approach advocated here encompasses a much broader array of assessment activities than is often envisioned.

Job and Person Analyses

The second step of our model involves conducting a job analysis on the one hand and then conducting a person analysis on the other. While these two activities are conceptualized as a single step, they are sufficiently different to justify separating our descriptions of the two.

Job Analysis. It should be obvious to even the most casual observer of the assessment process that any competent assessment requires a job analysis to determine the necessary competencies for success on that particular job. A thorough job analysis involves a description of work activities involved in the job, that is, what the incumbent actually does in the job and the competencies necessary to carry out activities successfully. A job analysis is always necessary to justify hiring decisions against claims of discriminatory hiring practices.

While it is beyond the scope of this manual to review the many approaches to job analysis, it is imperative for those involved in individual assessment to have a clear understanding of the competencies required for success in any given job. Quite simply, if you are not sure about what you are looking for, you will never know when you find it! Appendix C provides a brief introduction to the process of job analysis that should help readers to understand this process better.

The job analysis allows us to establish competency specifications for that job—specifications that drive the individual assessment process. They inform us about what kind of measures we need to use in the person analysis; they establish the level of the knowledge, skills, and abilities (KSAs) that we will be seeking as we assess various individuals; they provide the foundation for our conclusions and recommendations; and they determine the structure of the final report.

A sample of a competency specification for an entry-level job based on job analysis appears in Exhibit 2.1 on page 20. Detailed specifications for the First-Line Manager/Supervisor and the Management/Executive positions appear in Appendices D and E, respectively. These specifications appear in questionnaire format, along with the necessary instructions for using the Job Analysis Questionnaire (JAQ) to identify the competencies necessary to fill actual jobs.

Person Analysis. The analysis of the person begins with a review of the job analysis. What are the competencies that are critical for this position? Once these characteristics are clearly in mind, the assessor then must determine how best to measure them. A wide range of approaches is available for any given individual assessment, from a minimal qualifications evaluation to a comprehensive, in-depth study of the individual and how well he or she fit the template provided by the job analysis.

The approach chosen should be determined by an informal cost/benefit analysis, weighing the costs of time and effort involved, of both the assessor and the individual being evaluated, against the benefits of greater understanding. For example, one of our clients, the HR manager of an amusement park, was responsible for recruiting and hiring 3,000 minimum-wage, summer employees in a six-week window of opportunity. Clearly this is a case for which only a minimum qualifications evaluation was possible, that is, where the job was described as realistically as possible—the so-called realistic job preview—followed by a review of the applicant's resume and a short, focused behavioral interview. While the accuracy of such a brief person analysis is far from perfect, the downside risks are modest and unsuccessful hires usually are readily replaced.

When we need to perform a person analysis with senior managers and executives, the issues involved become quite complex. How do we assess the capacity for strategic thinking, for visionary leadership, for decision making, and the other necessary attributes to succeed at the top of an organization? While there are measures that provide clues about the degree to which a person possesses these qualities, assessing them requires a considerable degree of knowledge and skill, which is why working with such individuals is typically reserved for the highest level of assessment competence.

Integration and Interpretation

As the next step in the process, the data obtained from the person analysis is integrated and compared to the template provided by the job analysis, leading to a recommendation to the final decision maker(s). This is ordinarily provided in a written report that may be augmented by an oral presentation. It should be understood that all too often the recommendation made in the individual assessment report becomes the decision; thus such recommendations should be made with this understanding in mind. The future of a real live person rests in our hands, and we need to be very aware of the magnitude of that responsibility. The focus of each integration and interpretation should always be on answering the critical question of how well this person's competencies match those required for on-the-job success.

Reporting the Results

Only under rare circumstances is the assessor the final decision maker about the future course of action(s) to be taken as the outcome of the individual assessment. Whether the assessor is an employee of the organization in which the assessments are being done or an external consultant, it is useful to identify these decision makers or end users as *clients*. Working with or for a client always suggests that a professional relationship exists between the service provider and the client. In working with clients, the provider, in this case the assessor, is expected to offer his or her best professional judgment and not shape either the data or the recommendations simply to please the client. Usually the assessor is responsible for providing the decision maker(s) with a relatively

Exhibit 2.1. Entry-Level Competency Model

This very basic entry-level competency model reflecting the minimalist approach has five components.

A. Does the person work effectively with other people?

This Work Activity (WA) involves initiating contact with co-workers or associates, recognizing and responding to questions or instructions from other people, remaining alert to cues from the environment, and attending to those cues to respond appropriately and productively.

The associated competencies include the ability to read simple instructions for information, which *may* require spoken and/or written literacy, and the ability to recognize and accommodate requests for service or assistance required or expected in personal service roles.

B. Can the individual learn new material?

This WA includes examples such as performing production operations in manufacturing or assembly activities, coding and recording data, counting materials for inventory, or completing working forms or production records.

The associated competencies include ability to estimate time and space of observed objects, ability to make choices that affect the security or well-being of others, and the ability to solve problems involving relatively few concrete principles or methods.

C. Can the individual do basic arithmetic?

This component is quantitative in nature. Examples of WA include maintaining checklists, logs, or worksheets, recording changes in operating systems records, verifying the accuracy of data in a computer file, or completing forms by filling in information such as numbers, time, equipment, and functioning status.

The associated competencies include the ability to make estimates, to transcribe numerical information, to perform basic arithmetic operations, and to understand the procedures in codes used to enter, change, or delete computer data.

D. Can the individual solve basic physical world-related work problems?

Typical WA in this category include performing production operations that involve the use of machine controls, placing material in a manufacturing process and actuating machine operations, inspecting products to detect errors, and troubleshooting and repairing simple mechanical equipment.

The associated competencies in problem solving include making choices or decisions following simple rules or procedures and the ability to operate hand-operated tools or implements to perform operations requiring accuracy.

E. Finally, is the individual willing to follow instructions and directions?

This WA involves following instructions, observing and following examples provided by others to complete WAs and accommodate priorities completing WAs, as well as providing information to others, answering questions, and so on.

The associated competencies include the ability to pace work activities and maintain a level of attention to detail essential to complete work assignments, the ability to adjust schedules to accommodate changes, and the ability to adapt to the conditions of the work and organization.

formal report on the nature of the assessment, how the individual performed, and, on the basis of this performance, what conclusions and recommendations were reached.

Follow-Up and Program Evaluation

If the individual assessment process is to be of value to the organization, some form of follow-up and evaluation will typically be necessary and useful. The purpose of the follow-up is to determine whether the time and resources used to assess potential employees is actually paying off. Among the questions that might be asked in such a follow-up is how often the recommendations emerging from the assessment process have been followed and how well these individuals fared as a result. While such questions are probably best answered by a formal research study, in many cases it simply is impossible to conduct a formal study, due to the small size of the sample, the lack of resources, and so on. But much can be learned by exercising an inquisitive mind and asking the right questions.

Moreover, it is important to remember that jobs and organizations change, and an assessment protocol that is on target one year may be outdated and in need of revision one or two years later. We must use the follow-up phase to inquire and track not only the usefulness of the individual assessments but also what is happening in the organization, in specific jobs, in the business in which the organization operates, and so on. Some follow-up would seem to be a requirement for those who conduct assessments, both internally and externally.

We will return to this model of the individual assessment process in Chapter Four, where we provide our views on how each step of this process should be applied.

Information Technology and Individual Assessment

The approach to testing and assessment as described in the previous section may be undergoing significant change. This change results from the use of information technology in general and the personal computer specifically. A description of the nature and importance of these changes on the science and art of individual assessment follows.

The History of Information Technology and Assessment

While the computer has been used for more than half a century to score and profile data from such tests as the Scholastic Aptitude Test (SAT) and the American College Test (ACT), such usage does not involve either the test taker or the recipient of the testing information in any direct fashion. Rather, a main-frame computer scores the test responses, typically by scanning a specially designed answer sheet according to an algorithm, and then produces a profile based on previously developed norms. Copies of the obtained results are then mailed to both parties. The invention and widespread adoption of the personal computer (PC), however, provides new technology.

Initially, the administration of a test on a PC required the test administrator to have purchased a computer disk (CD) containing the test items and then to have purchased from the test publisher the authorization to score and profile the test responses. To test an individual, the test administrator would first insert the CD in the PC, reboot the PC, and, after the testing was completed, access the scoring and profiling algorithm and run this second portion of the program. While this process was an improvement over the paper-and-pencil administration, it was still regarded as somewhat cumbersome and difficult. Thus, computer-based testing had only a minor impact of the field of assessment. This changed, however, with the development of the Internet and the World-Wide Web.

The past two decades have seen a tremendous growth of the Internet. It is estimated that by the end of 2002 over 600 million persons worldwide had regular Internet access, either at home or at work (*Encyclopedia Britannica,* 2005.) One consequence of this Internet access has been the growth of availability and convenience in the delivery of psychological assessments, dramatically increasing the use of computers in psychological assessment. The computer can now deliver the test directly to the test taker, score the responses, produce a profile of the scores, and also often deliver a narrative report explaining the test results, sometimes in elaborate detail—all via the Internet. While the test administrator must have purchased the right to use the testing program, this is usually done once. The test administrator may then be automatically charged for each use of the test or may have purchased an unrestricted usage license.

Thus the PC now enables the assessor to provide easy access to testing around the clock, immediate scoring and profiling of test responses, and some degree of automated test interpretation—all of which are of considerable advantage in the assessment process. It has also been argued by some that the anonymity of computer-based non-cognitive tests promotes greater candor and openness. On the other hand, serious questions have been raised about the integrity of computer-administered tests, that is, how do we know the true identity of the test taker and how do we monitor the various forms of cheating. And there is a critical question of the equivalence of computer-based and paper-and-pencil-based test administrations. Each of these issues will be addressed below. It should be noted that we are restricting our discussion to tests administered in a professional context by human resources specialists, psychologists, and other trained persons and have excluded the many tests available on the Internet for self-analysis and personal enlightenment.

Computer Delivery of Assessments

One of the singular advantages of testing individuals on a computer is that the assessment can be completed any time a computer is available to the test taker, which greatly enhances the availability of tests for a wide variety of uses, including both pre-employment evaluations and planning for training and development. Tests that can be taken at any time and place are no longer restricted to the human resources officer's or psychologist's office.

Nevertheless, this convenience comes at a price. How can we be certain that the person providing the answers is the same person we are considering as a job applicant? And does taking the test online produce a different result from using a traditional paper-and-pencil version of the same test? Several methods exist to prevent others from taking a test for an applicant, the most common of which is supervising the applicant and requiring photo identification. But this process, of course, reduces the convenience of online testing, which is its *raison d'etre*. A more promising approach is to use a keyboard that includes a fingerprint reader that prevents anyone else from taking the test. Unfortunately, this technology is not yet widely available and, consequently, test administrators need to be sensitive to the possibility of fraudulent test taking.

Equivalence of Computer-Based and Conventional Testing

There is a substantial body of empirical research on the equivalence of tests administered by computer and by the more traditional paper-and-pencil method. By and large, this body of research (Buchanan, Goldberg, & Johnson, 1999; Campbell, Rohlman, Storzbach, Binder, Anger, Kovera, Davis, & Grossman, 1999; DiLalla, 1996; Nouman & Baydoun, 1998) clearly shows that the online versions of most of the *personality* tests have the same psychometric characteristics as their paper-and-pencil versions and that scores on the two forms of the tests from the same group of persons are highly correlated. These researchers have concluded that the two versions of the personality tests studied were roughly equivalent to each other. Certain variations in the factorial structure of the two versions, however, lead to a temporizing of these conclusions and to the recommendation that additional validation of the online version of any personality test requires new validation.

The picture for the equivalence of *cognitive ability* tests, however, is more mixed. Coynes, Warszta, and Beadle (2005) also included a measure of cognitive ability in their carefully counterbalanced study and found that the scores from the online version of the cognitive ability measure were significantly lower than those from the traditional paper-and-pencil version, differences that could not be ascribed to the presence or absence of supervision of the test nor to whether the test was delivered online or by a CD. In a meta-analysis of the equivalence of tests of cognitive ability, Mead and Drasgow (1993) found that while power tests (those without time limits) were highly equivalent, speed tests (those with time limits) were less equivalent. Meta-analysis is a statistical process that evaluates the common findings from a variety of different published research studies. Specifically, their meta-analysis revealed that, while the psychometric properties of the two versions were the same, the average scores on the computerized versions were lower than those on the paper-and-pencil versions.

These findings have been replicated by Van de Vijer, Fons, and Harsfeldt (1994), who found that the results from the computer version of the General Aptitude Test Battery, a widely used test of various abilities, were lower than those from the conventional version and that this trend was strongest for simple clerical tasks. A recent unpublished study by the authors found that there were no differences between the two *untimed* versions of a clerical ability test, supporting the notion that the computer version of simple speed tests is more difficult for test takers than the paper-and-pencil version. But these findings all lead to the conclusion that, while the two versions of most cognitive tests are more-or-less equivalent, there is a need for separate norms for each of the versions in order to take the different difficulty levels of the two versions into account. We will return to this issue in Chapter Four.

Users of the Internet for testing need to be aware of the caveats about the potential technical and ethical problems inherent in such testing identified by a special American Psychological Association task force (Naglieri, Drasgow, Schmitt, Handler, Prifitera, Margolis, & Velasquez, 2004). These concerns include maintaining the integrity of the test, providing test security, ensuring that special populations such as persons with disabling conditions and those from linguistically and culturally different groups are properly included, and, finally, assuring that appropriate norms are available for such tests—all issues that we have touched on previously.

Candor and Computer-Based Personality Tests

Does computer administration of personality tests produce greater openness and candor on the part of test takers? While there is some indication (for example, Davis, 1999; Wallace, 1999) that the impersonal nature of taking a personality test on the computer does produce less defensiveness, Potosky and Bobko (1997) found the opposite to be true. It is thus difficult to know whether there are any systematic differences in how test takers respond emotionally to these two different modes of test presentation.

It should be noted that one might argue that the degree of openness may be a function of the intent of the personality test. Taking such a test on a computer as part of a research study is quite a different process from taking a personality assessment instrument, where "putting one's best foot forward" is implicit. Our own experience in developing personality tests for employment screening is that scales intended to measure response distortion, that is, positive impression management, are significantly higher than those obtained in research studies. Further, there are highly significant differences between employed individuals and applicants on such scales, with applicants clearly giving more socially desirable responses, even those that are highly implausible, such as "I have never told a lie, even to spare the feelings of a friend." While not unique to computer-based versions of personality tests, attempting to present the most positive image of one's self is an inescapable part of pre-employment testing.

Interpretation and Integration of Test Results

Online tests have a variety of approaches to test interpretation, ranging from a simple reporting of the numerical test scores and their percentile equivalents to elaborate narrative discussions of the presumed meaning of the scores. Indeed, some well-regarded testing programs yield reports of twenty or more pages describing the personal/interpersonal characteristics of the test taker in some detail. These narrative descriptions are usually based on pooled expert judgments about the meaning of both individual personality test scores and various patterns of such scores.

While such descriptions are often quite useful in helping the assessor understand the nature of the person as measured by that particular test, no program presently available can integrate the results of more than one test. Even more importantly, these interpretative programs cannot assess the degree of match between the person and the job requirements—the all-important person-job match that sets a limit on the usefulness of these interpretations. Thus we find ourselves in agreement with Butcher, Perry, and Atlis (2000), who conclude their review of the validity and utility of computer-based test interpretation as follows:

". . .computer-generated reports should be viewed as valuable adjuncts to, rather than substitutes for, clinical judgments." (p. 15)

We will return to this issue in Chapter Five.

IT and Assessment: A Summary

Given the above considerations, how important has the impact of IT been on the practice of individual assessment? There is no question that IT has simplified and eased the delivery of tests, especially the scoring and profiling of tests that previously required time-consuming hand scoring, but the fundamental issues of individual assessment remain. The competencies to be measured through assessments must rest on a careful job analysis; the measures used, regardless of how they are delivered, need to be both reliable and valid for the purpose for which they are being used (Barak & English, 2002; Buchanan, 2002); appropriate norms need to be selected; and the integration of the results must result in a carefully developed and balanced picture of the person being assessed.

Problems of the identity of the test taker and the more general problem of the security of the Internet have not been completely resolved. Thus, we must conclude that, outside of making tests more available and convenient, the model of individual assessment carefully presented previously in this chapter still is the necessary model for practitioners to follow.

Summary

To summarize and emphasize some of the key points of Chapter Two, keep in mind that the practice of individual assessment is conducted in both the private and public sectors. Individual assessment is not the exclusive domain of industrial/organizational psychologists; many human resources staff members and even some line managers do such assessments as well. One of the key points is that the approach to the individual assessment process presented here is a very systematic, functional approach to gathering data about an individual and a specific job. In the interest of accuracy and usefulness, it is essential that this systematic approach include:

- Organization and work-setting analysis;
- Job analysis utilizing multiple sources;
- Analysis of the applicant using the resume, interview, testing, small job sampling, and other relevant data sources;
- Analysis, integration, and cross-checking data;
- Thorough reporting of the results; and
- Follow-up and program evaluation.

These features are essential, both to ensure compliance with legal standards of job relatedness and to improve the accuracy and utility of any decision. They should be the criteria the end user employs in evaluating the quality of the assessment products that have been contracted. Another approach to evaluating the products received is to compare them with the samples from our practice provided in Appendices F through H.

Finally, changes in the process of individual assessment resulting from recent developments in information technology are described, together with questions raised by some of these new technologies.

Before we examine the process of individual assessment in greater detail, in the next chapter we detour for a brief discussion of the principles of psychological measurement, which provide the foundation of the assessment process. Functioning effectively as a professional practitioner in this field requires some grasp of these basic concepts.

Chapter Three

Psychological Measurement

Before we discuss the various types of psychological tests and some specific tests that are typically used in individual assessment, it is imperative that we review the essentials of psychometrics—the principles of measurement that underlie all psychological tests— the foundations of the field of individual assessment. These principles include the normal distribution curve, reliability, validity, and norms. While we assume that many readers will be quite familiar with these concepts, their importance to understanding the overall assessment process makes such a review essential.

The Normal Distribution Curve

The normal distribution curve—the bell-shaped curve—is the basis of virtually all psychological testing and most of the statistical procedures that are used to evaluate test data. The normal distribution curve was initially developed by Abraham DeMoivre (1667–1754), a French-born, English mathematician, based on his studies of the probabilities involved in gambling. The first scientist to attempt to apply the normal distribution curve to human characteristics was Adolph Quetelet (1796–1874), a Belgian scientist, who found that both the chest measurements of Scottish soldiers and heights of French soldiers were normally distributed. Quetelet's Body Mass Index (BMI), another normally distributed variable, is still in use today. Following Quetelet, decades of empirical research have supported the conclusion that most human characteristics are normally distributed.

All normal distribution curves are bell-shaped and symmetrical (identical halves). As we can see in Figure 3.1 on the next page, the tails of the curve approach the x or horizontal axis but never reach it; instead the curve goes on to infinity in both directions. It is also important to note that, in a perfect normal curve, the mean (arithmetic average), the median (the mid-point of the distribution), and the mode (the most frequent datum) all would have the same value.

As we move away from the mean and we divide the distribution into equal segments along the x axis, we can see that each of these segments, or standard deviations, encompasses a smaller number of cases and that + three standard deviations accounts for 99.7 percent of all the data. The majority of the scores, 68 percent, cluster around the mean, and the more extreme scores are spread out along the x axis in ever-decreasing numbers.

As we also can see from Figure 3.1, dividing the x or horizontal axis into equal occurring units in a given distribution produces percentile equivalents. To actually determine the percentile equivalent of any given data point, we would convert the data point into a z score, which simply tells us how many units or standard deviations that data point is from the mean. The formula to determine a z score for a given data point is a simple one: z = data point − mean/standard deviation of that distribution. For example, if we have a calculated z score of 1.43 for a particular data point, we can readily determine, using a table of z scores, that a z score of 1.43 is equivalent to .0764 of the total distribution, or that approximately 92 percent of the distribution falls below that data point, or that this data point is at the 92nd percentile.

The implications of this brief review of the normal distribution curve for psychological testing are clear. Psychological test scores are normally distributed so that there are as many below-average scores as there are above-average scores. Indeed, when this is not the case, the test developers use a variety of statistical techniques to "normalize" the distribution. Only in mythical Lake Woebegone are "all the children above average."

Figure 3.1. The Normal Distribution Curve

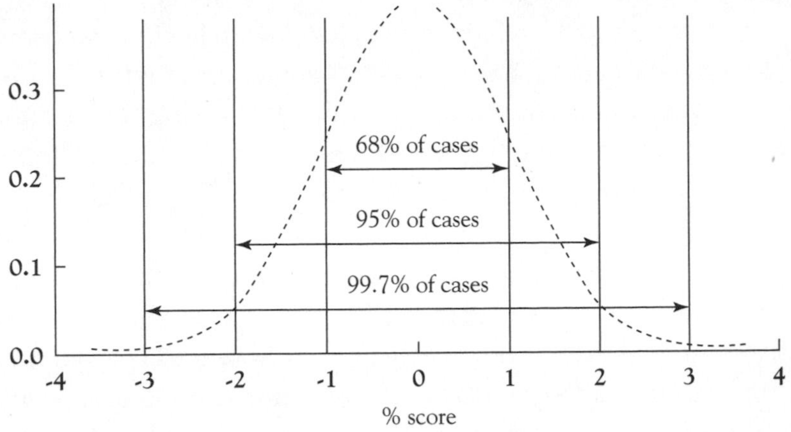

Reliability

Reliability refers to the consistency, the trustworthiness, of a measurement. There are no perfect measures of anything. All our measuring instruments are fallible, as are the people who use them. In many instances we recognize this lack of consistency and make allowances for it. For example, we know that the old grandfather clock in our hall tends to run slow toward the end of the week, just before we need to wind it again, and we make the appropriate correction in our understanding of the accurate time. Not every time piece is connected to the Naval Observatory atomic clock that is accurate to the hundredths of a second, and even it is off by a tiny amount, that's not enough for most of us to care about. But if we were timing the speed of a subatomic particle, we might care a great deal.

We need to understand the accuracy of any measuring instrument that we use so that we can make the appropriate correction. Political pollsters usually provide us with such information when they report their polling results. Thus, when they report that candidate X has 46 percent of the potential votes while candidate Y has only 43 percent, with the remaining 11 percent "undecided," with a 4 percent error of measurement, we know immediately that this race is "still up for grabs."

Turning now to the reliability of psychological tests, we recognize that such tests are also subject to errors of measurement that lower their reliability or consistency. The individual taking the test may not have been paying full attention, may not have cared about a good performance, or was simply having a "bad day." If we compare two or more different tests of the same characteristics, we see that the items are different, the scoring systems are not the same, and fatigue may have influenced the individual as he or she went from test to test. And sheer luck in guessing the answers also plays a role.

If we examine test results over an extended period of time and find differences, are these differences due to changes in the individual or are they an artifact of the testing process? Answering such questions is critical to understanding an individual and coming to any conclusion about that person. Is this person really less depressed than he was six weeks ago, suggesting the medications are helping, or is the lowered score on the depression scale a reflection of its low reliability? Has this person really developed the necessary skill to do the job, or is her improved test score a function of a disruptive environment in the initial testing? Clearly, how these questions are answered has significant implications for the individual and, over time, reflects on the usefulness of tests in the assessment process.

It should be noted that test scores will change over time due to training, experience, and general education. Such changes are especially noticeable over time in tests of job skills and problem-solving ability. Further, test scores are subject to change as a result of re-testing, which typically leads to slight increases in scores as a function of familiarization, specific on-the-job training where knowledge is acquired, and personal maturation, which is most apparent in young adults as they learn from life's experiences. These trends tend to impact some tests more than others, and assessors should carefully review test manuals for information about such trends. Assessors need to be cognizant of such trends and take them into account in interpreting test results.

When concerns about the reliability of a measure are raised, steps can be taken to address them. Such concerns do arise when a test result is out of range of expected findings. The test can be re-administered; if available, an alternative form of the test can be used or a similar test can be substituted. Any of these steps can help resolve questions about the role of the reliability of the test in understanding the obtained results.

As we earlier noted, there are no perfect measuring instruments and thus no perfectly reliable psychological tests. What alternatives are open to us? As with our grandfather clock or the political polls, if we know what corrections we need to make in our obtained measure to estimate the true measure, then we can proceed, albeit with some degree of caution. In more technical terms, if we know the *error of measurement*, we can better estimate the *true score*. While we find the phrase *error of measurement* an unfortunate one, suggesting that a mistake has been made rather than that we have identified a natural aspect of all measurement, this is the term that is typically used in measurement texts and psychological test manuals.

One of the major ways that psychological tests differ from other measuring instruments is that responsible test developers are knowledgeable about these errors of measurement and typically are meticulous in their efforts to identify and reduce them. When they have done all that it is possible to do, they report the remaining errors of measurement in the technical manuals that routinely accompany such tests. The failure to report such information or the unwillingness of a test vendor to freely provide such data is a strong warning about the quality of that instrument. We wish that the providers of other measuring procedures, especially in medicine, were as thorough in addressing errors of measurement.

Estimating Reliability

The reliability of a psychological test is typically addressed in at least one of four ways: (1) internal consistency; (2) equivalence; (3) stability or test-retest; and (4) split-half reliability. Each of these methods provides an estimate of this important property of a test. Which of these estimates is the best fit, however, depends on the use to which the test and its scores will be put.

The internal consistency of the test involves a determination of the extent to which all the test items are assessing the same construct or variable. Internal consistency is most commonly assessed with a statistic termed Cronbach's *alpha*. A Cronbach alpha of .80 or above is regarded as good support for the reliability of the test or scale. An earlier version of this approach used the Kuder-Richardson Formula 20, which is now rarely used.

The equivalence approach to reliability involves administering two different, but equivalent, forms of the test at the same time to a group of subjects and correlating the obtained scores. When this approach is used, half of the subjects are given one form first and the other half of the subjects receives the alternative form first. Then the process is reversed. Since developing even a single form of a test is arduous and time-consuming, alternate forms often are not available and thus this approach is little used. This approach is used when there may be questions about test security or simply questions about the construct being measured.

The third method of obtaining reliability—test-retest— involves administering the same test on two or more separate occasions and computing the correlations between the score obtained on each administration. In measuring the reliability of an instrument using the test-retest method, it should be recognized that a practice effect may cause some increase in the mean scores over administrations, but retesting should not affect the correlations between the two distributions. For both the equivalence and the test-retest method, the expected size of the obtained correlations should be at least .80, and preferably higher.

The fourth method of estimating reliability is the split-half method, where the reliability is estimated by correlating the score obtained on one half of the items with that from the other half and then using the Spearman-Brown prophecy formula to estimate the reliability. Usually the odd-numbered items are compared with the even-numbered items, especially if the items are randomly placed in the test. This method requires the assumption of homogeneity of item content.

As we have noted, there is no perfectly reliable measuring tool—of any kind. When we are assessing candidates for important roles in an organization, it seems appropriate to use more than a single measure to assess a critical competence. For example, we may wish to use more than one measure of personality, perhaps one based on the five-factor approach and another that focuses more directly on leadership attributes. Using such multiple measures both gives us different views of the individual and also helps reduce the inherent unreliability of a single instrument.

Obviously, reliability is an important characteristic of any test that we choose to use for prediction. The scores that we obtain from our assessments need to be trustworthy, but the fundamental basis for choosing a test is validity—whether or not we can interpret our findings soundly and whether or not the test results suit our purpose. We now turn our attention to this critical issue of validity. However, we hasten to note here that the validity of any measuring instrument is contingent on its reliability. If an instrument is not reliable, all measures obtained from that instrument are meaningless. No amount of tinkering with such an instrument can reveal truth when none is available. This fact is equally true for measures used in individual assessment.

Validity

The validity of psychological tests can best be defined as the truthfulness of the test, that is, whether accurate predictions about an individual can be made on the basis of his or her scores on that test. Of course, no universal test exists that enables us to predict all the behaviors of an individual. Thus, when we ask about the validity of a test, the question boils down to whether the test can predict the behaviors that it purports to predict. For example, does a data-entry aptitude test predict how well a person can perform as a data-entry operator? Does this test of personality help us understand how well this person gets along with people or how effectively she can work on a team? We need to be clear that the validity of a test always must be considered in the context of what behavior(s) it is intended to predict.

Types of Validity

In general, there are three ways of evaluating the validity or predictive usefulness of a psychological test—content, predictive, and construct validity. *Content validity*, sometimes referred to as *face validity*, refers to the extent to which the test items directly represent the content of the behavior being assessed. For example, an honesty/integrity test should directly inquire about the test taker's relevant past behaviors such as filching supplies, falsifying a resume, and so on; while a supervisory skills test should tap those skills necessary to succeed as a supervisor. Our Test of Supervisory Skills (Prien & Goodstein, 2004), for example, presents the test taker with a list of behaviors that supervisors have been known to engage in and asks him or her to rate each of these behaviors as either *ineffective, neutral,* or *effective*. The scoring key was based on the result of previous studies that had shown either a positive or a negative correlation between that behavior and rating of supervisory success. Those items with a positive correlation are keyed as effective, those with no correlation are scored as neutral, and those with a negative relationship between that behavior and success are keyed as ineffective.

Predictive validity, sometimes termed criterion-related validity, refers to the extent to which a measure is related to behavioral measures of the target characteristic, obtained either concurrently or in the future. Thus, the honesty/integrity test scores should predict such behaviors as theft, dishonest time reporting, and the like, either concurrently or in the short-term future, and the Test of Supervisory Skills (TOSS) would need to predict success as a supervisor. Indeed, later research has shown that TOSS does predict supervisory success in a variety of industrial settings. It should be noted that, despite appearances, some tests with apparent high content validity, for example, the several tests of creativity, do *not* have predictive validity. This is critically important, as predictive validity is typically regarded as the gold standard in evaluating tests because a test that has predictive value does have clear-cut usefulness.

Validity may also be seen as an overall evaluative judgment of the degree to which both the research evidence and the theory support the "adequacy and appropriateness of interpretations and actions on the basis of test scores or other modes of assessment" (Messick, 1995, p. 741). Messick goes on to point out that since the validity of a test is a judgmental issue, it is always evolving—and thus validation must always be a continuing process. For example, although the Minnesota Multiphasic Personality Test (MMPI) is over sixty years old, validation research continues to be published, adding to our understanding of the meaning of scores on that instrument.

Benchmarking is frequently used to establish concurrent validity by identifying specific behavioral characteristics associated with scores on a psychological test battery, that is, the relationships between measures collected at the same time. It is often important to supplement this concurrent validity by conducting a predictive validity study, that is, does the test predict *future* behavior, to determine how robust the particular test or battery might be. We will provide a more detailed account of the benchmarking process in Chapter Four.

Construct validity is the most difficult concept to explain briefly; nevertheless, we shall try. Many tests purport to measure concepts for which there is no single, specific criterion against which to correlate the test scores. Intelligence, ego strength, and artistic ability are but a few examples of such concepts. Construct validity involves the gradual accumulation of supporting empirical evidence gathered from a variety of sources that confirms the generally understood meaning of the concept and supports the use of tests that measure that concept.

If we take intelligence as an example, more than a century of research clearly has supported that intelligence tests are useful in predicting a wide variety of "intelligent" behaviors such as academic achievement, success in training programs, on-the-job success, and lifetime achievement and income. Research on typical intelligence tests, which heavily tap verbal fluency and problem solving, provides overwhelming evidence supporting the usefulness of intelligence testing for predicting a broad variety of important workplace behaviors.

In general, validity may be considered as the degree to which evidence supports the inferences and predictions made from test scores. This is the single most important consideration in choosing a psychological test for an individual assessment. Not only must the test be reliable, but also required is adequate evidence that the test under consideration will yield data that will increase our understanding of this individual, especially in the situation for which he or she is being considered. While both the reliability and validity of a test, especially the latter, are critical to which test we choose to use, the availability of appropriate norms is a third critical consideration.

Norms

Norms are the empirically derived distribution of scores on a test. These data sets allow us to compare an obtained score with those from a comparable group of other test takers. Without appropriate norms, it is impossible to know the meaning of an obtained raw score; we need to be able to translate that score into a percentile equivalent or some type of a standard score, such as a z score, in order to determine where this individual stands in relation to his or her peers.

Many measurements do not require norms for interpretation. When told that a room is 10 feet by 12 feet, most of us visualize the size of that room. But if we were given the size in meters, many of us would be unsure of its size. The Old Testament provides an even more telling example. Not only did God instruct Noah to build an ark, but he specified its dimensions—its length was to be 300 cubits, its breadth 50 cubits, and its height 30 cubits. How big was Noah's ark? The answer depends on whether or not you can translate a cubit into a more common unit of measurement. Once you learn that a cubit is the length from the crook of the elbow to the furthest fingertip, about 18 inches for a contemporary, aging, male psychologist, we can answer the question. The ark was approximately 450 feet long, 75 feet across, and 45 feet high—clearly large enough for all the animals, two by two!

With the single exception of individually administered intelligence tests, other psychological tests require reference to a table of norms for that test to interpret individual scores. Going back to the original Stanford-Binet Intelligence Test in 1916, such tests have established a mean Intelligence Quotient (IQ) of 100 and a standard deviation of 15 points. Based on the normal distribution curve discussed above, we know that an IQ of 115 (one standard deviation above the mean) exceeds 84 percent of the population. That is, experienced psychologists are as familiar with the meaning of an obtained IQ as they are with feet and inches.

Most other psychological test scores, however, require a table of norms to decode the meaning of any obtained individual score. The most useful norms will allow us to compare an obtained score with a relevant norm group. Thus, if we are testing for data-entry skills, the most useful sets of norms would be applicants for a data-entry position. When testing applicants for sales positions for a large ladies ready-to-wear company, the most useful sets of norms would be obtained from applicants for similar jobs with similar businesses. Failing that, we would have to settle for a norm base of sales personnel in a range of businesses. But it should be clear that the degree to which the norm group that we use differs from the situation for which we want to predict, the accuracy of our prediction is probably lessened. Thus the most useful tests in any given situation are those that allow us to compare the individual we are assessing with groups of individuals in the *most* similar situations.

The Role of the Assessor

To return to the question of the validity of assessment measurements and of the assessment process as a whole, validity depends not only on the validity of the tests themselves but also on how the assessment data is collected and interpreted. The assessor's knowledge and skill in pulling together disparate, and sometime contradictory, information determines the quality and the usefulness of the final report. This clinical-level understanding comes about only through extensive experience and over time. Meanwhile, there are less sophisticated approaches to data interpretation.

Assessment data is collected both mechanically and clinically, and that data is processed using both mechanical and clinical procedures. That is, tests can be administered, scored, and profiled using computer- or web-based programs or by individuals who execute these functions. The advantages of using the electronic-based means of data collection are uniformity, speed, and accuracy; the disadvantage is that there is no opportunity for a trained professional to observe the individual being assessed and include these impressions as part of the total assessment process, although this usually does occur as part of the interviewing process.

In either case, however, there is usually a need for a final or summary report that includes the assessor's recommendations about courses of action to pursue. In drafting such a report, the *assessor* becomes an *instrument of assessment* and *prediction*. Thus, in the final analysis, the key element in the assessment process is the assessor himself or herself. Regardless of how the assessment information is collected, an assessor must synthesize this information into a comprehensive picture of the individual from which predictions about that individual can be made.

At the lowest level of assessment, the assessment information can be combined mechanically; formulae can be developed that yield a prediction—a reasonable solution when large numbers of candidates need to be assessed for rather simple tasks. The highest level of practice, evaluating candidates for senior management or executive positions, for example, requires the most sophisticated strategy-capturing models and the use of complex, professional judgment. However, regardless of the level of professional expertise required and used, the assessment process is a rational process. We are not making guesses about individuals; rather, we are using data-gathering instruments and then combining those data to arrive at a characterization of the individual.

A basic premise of this approach is that a wide variety of psychological tests and measurements can provide useful information about individuals. While the statement is not true of all tests available in the market, those tests that are constructed following standard psychometric principles followed by empirical research and evaluation have the potential to yield trustworthy data. For the most part, people behave in ways that are consistent with their performance and self-description on tests and other psychological measurements. Furthermore, the data from an individual's test performance and self-description can be used to make inferences about that person's future behavior in work and organization settings. While the majority of individuals put their best feet forward in an assessment setting, that degree of faking can be either controlled or accounted for when interpreting test performance.

After an extensive review on the validity of assessments based on psychological tests that had been reported in 125 published meta-analyses based on eight hundred unique samples, Meyer, Finn, Eyde, Kay, Moreland, Dies, Eisman, Kubiszyn, and Reed (2001) concluded that the validity of psychological tests is "strong and compelling" (p. 128). They further concluded that the validity of psychological tests is comparable to that of medical tests and that such tests provide distinct, unique sources of data about people that is not obtainable from interviews alone. But they also noted that the process of extracting the critical information from a battery of tests is not a simple one, but one that requires a "high degree of skill and sophistication to be implemented properly" (p. 144).

Classification of Psychological Tests

The psychological tests and measurement tools used in individual assessment fall into four major groups or categories: (1) measures of personal/interpersonal characteristics, the so-called personality tests; (2) specific job competency tests; (3) measures of cognitive ability; and (4) miscellaneous, various tests of a type that are insufficiently numerous to warrant an independent category. Most individual assessment tests are included in one of these four types, each of which is covered below. Our discussion is limited to the types of tests available, not to any specific tests. Appendix I provides a listing of selected tests in each of these four categories, together with information about the publisher of that instrument.

Tests of Personal/Interpersonal Characteristics

Extensive information about individuals can be obtained through personality tests or measures describing social and personal functioning, including patterns of interests and work style. Here, our focus is on questionnaire measures, where the individual chooses or endorses various items of self-description. There have been a number of significant reviews of the usefulness of personality tests used in assessment and prediction in the research literature. While the early findings were quite discouraging about the usefulness of such instruments in the workplace, that conclusion has been radically changed with the development of personality tests based on the so-called five-factor approach to personality measurement. The research on the usefulness of interest and work style inventories is less supportive of their use in the workplace.

The "Big Five" factors—neuroticism, extroversion, openness to new experience, agreeableness, and conscientiousness—have been shown routinely to be highly useful in predicting a number of work and organizational behaviors (Barrick & Mount, 1991, 1993; Costa & McRae, 1992a, 1992b, 1992c; Digman, 1990; Goldberg, 1982a, 1982b, 1993; Goodstein & Lanyon, 1999; McRae & Costa, 1987,

1990; Tett, Jackson, & Rothstein, 1991). Not surprisingly, conscientiousness has emerged as the most consistent predictor of job performance of the big five factors, regardless of the type of performance measure used or the level of the job involved. People who were seen as the most conscientious by themselves and/or others were the most effective workers. Extraversion correlated well with success in training, but less well with job performance. Openness to new experience also correlated with job training, but not with later job performance, suggesting that being gregarious, outgoing, and curious were factors in success in training, but not in later job performance. Neither agreeableness nor neuroticism has been found to be routinely correlated with job success.

More importantly, studies have shown that, when personality measures used in selection have been selected on the basis of job analyses, these measures were more predictive of job success than those measures selected without such analyses. These studies strongly confirm the usefulness of using the five factors as predictors of on-the-job performance, particularly when the personality measures are selected on the basis of a job analysis. It should be obvious that extroversion, for example, is much more important for a salesperson or a customer service representative than for a data entry clerk.

In the practice of individual assessment, a cautious and skeptical approach to the use of personality or individual difference measures is justified and, indeed, warranted. There are literally hundreds of measures of individual personality characteristics. Many of these are unique and have been developed to fit a particular situation, and their general usefulness is open to question. Others are designed for the diagnosis of mental illness, rather than differentiating among normal individuals in the work setting. It is essential that individual assessment practitioners apply reasonable caution and follow accepted professional standards when they are selecting tests or other measurement tools. What this means is simply that the practitioner should possess some form of validity evidence to support the use of a test or other measure to describe or make predictions about the behavior of individuals in the work setting.

Substantial research support exists for the use of various personality measures in individual assessment, especially those more recently developed ones that are based on contemporary psychometric theory. An often-asked question is why these self-report measures are effective predictors of non-test behaviors. A simple answer is that most people behave in ways that are generally consistent across time and situations. Most normal people recognize these behavioral consistencies and are able to reliably report on them; they can and usually will say who they are! The catch is that what they "are" must be appreciated and understood. This understanding provides the basis for the individual assessment process and for making predictions about their current and future performance, as we will discuss further in subsequent sections of this guide.

Tests of Specific Job Competencies

In reviewing applicants for many jobs, it is imperative to know whether or not the applicant has the general or specific job skills(s) necessary to perform the job. Can this person perform routine clerical tasks speedily and accurately? How many error-free characters can this applicant enter into a database in an allotted time? Can this applicant follow simple oral directions? How well coordinated is this person? Can this person "close" a sale? Knowing the answers to such questions is as critical to the individual assessment process as are the applicant's personality characteristics. Fortunately, there are many available tests that can provide the answers to such questions. There are both generalized ability tests and tests that tap fairly specific jobs skills.

Among the various generalized ability or competency tests are measures of psychomotor ability, speed and accuracy, complex coordination, spatial visualization, two-hand coordination, and so on. Such generalized ability tests tap the aptitudes or skills that underlie the acquisition of those skills necessary to perform the job as well as later performance on these jobs.

In addition to these generalized skills tests, many tests of specific job skills exist, such as data entry, proofreading, operating a lathe, driving a forklift, and so on. These tests are often regarded as *work samples*, as they indeed evaluate the individual's performance on a sample of the job to be performed. Many of these measures of specific job skills have been developed by the organization that intends to use them, by employer groups, and by trade unions, especially for apprentice programs.

In choosing to use any measure of a specific job competency, a number of issues must be considered. The most important is whether the test actually taps a skill or some component of a skill that is important to success in the specific job that is under review. The optimal way to make such a decision is to determine the relationship between scores on that measure and job performance, that is, the validity of the test in this particular situation. But this is often not possible, for a variety of reasons, including a lack of time and resources as well as limitations in the size of an available sample to conduct such a validation study. Under such circumstances, we need to evaluate carefully the degree to which the normative sample described in the test manual resembles the population we are going to evaluate. The quality of the provided norms is also an important consideration. Do the available norms help us decide where an individual whom we are assessing really stands? For example, if we are interested in evaluating experienced machinists and the norms are based on the scores of trainees, this test will be of limited value to us.

Measures of Intellectual Functioning

Intellectual functioning, also known as general cognitive ability or general mental ability or intelligence, has long been understood to be an important determinant of success, both in school and on the job (McClelland, 1973; Schmidt, 2002; Schmidt & Hunter, 1998). The label "intelligence" has recently fallen into disuse in personnel settings because of its emotional impact on many people. In developing this assessment procedure, we have selected the term "cognitive ability" as a more neutral, user-friendly label, one without the excess baggage of the term "intelligence." We regard a measure of general cognitive ability as an assessment that combines two or more specific mental aptitudes, that is, an assessment that includes a variety of items measuring specific abilities (for example, verbal, spatial, and numerical) that are critical in the acquisition and utilization of information.

It is important to understand the significance of job complexity in predicting job success. In general, and not surprisingly, the more complex the job, the more important is general cognitive ability. These findings have been shown to hold true for a wide variety of jobs both in the United States and in Europe. Other demonstrations of the validity of tests of cognitive ability have involved contrasting the mean scores of persons belonging to various occupational groups. These mean scores show the relative rankings that would be expected on the basis of the complexity and intellectual difficulty of different occupations.

What is the nature and content of general mental ability? Much has been written on this topic. A review of this literature and of the content of a sample of existing tests shows that there are three basic types of items: verbal, numerical or quantitative, and spatial. This is a well-recognized system for classifying items on tests of general ability. Most of the individual measures of cognitive ability, such as the various versions of the individually administered Wechsler intelligence tests, as well as the various versions of the Stanford-Binet, contain a number of subtests that are scored and added to obtain an overall score. Most tests are based on the underlying premise that these subtests are components of a single concept, and therefore that the single overall score is the best estimate of cognitive function.

To summarize, the use of brief structured tests of general mental ability in personnel settings is now well established. An early study (Schippmann & Prien, 1989) demonstrated that a combination of a cognitive ability test and personality test measures could significantly predict managerial success in a variety of manufacturing and service setting. A meta-analysis of many research studies investigating the use of psychological tests in predicting success in employment situations has shown that optimal prediction across many types of settings is achieved by the use of a measure of the personality trait of conscientiousness in combination with a brief paper-and-pencil measure of general mental ability (Behling, 1998). Thus, a measure of mental ability should be an essential component of any competent personnel selection program.

Miscellaneous Tests

Included in this category are those tests that arguably do not conveniently fit into the first three categories, yet are potentially useful additions to the individual assessment process. Included in this miscellaneous category are tests of management and leadership, honesty and integrity, and creativity. While it can be argued that tests of management and leadership ability should be included in personality measures and measures of creativity in special ability, we regard these three sets of tests as sufficiently different as to be separated from the other three categories, but neither numerous nor central enough to merit individual categories; hence we lump them into a miscellaneous grouping.

Contemporary measures of management and leadership usually have been developed by comparing the questionnaire responses of managers and executives with those of line employees (that is, by using position level as a surrogate criterion) or by comparing the responses of highly successful managers and executives with those of less successful ones. Ratings of managerial and executive performance have also been used to validate such measures, and a more recent line of research has identified the characteristics of successful managers and executives who have been "derailed" in their careers. It is clear, at least to us, that such specially designed and empirically validated tests of management and leadership are much more appropriate to use with such individuals than the more generic personality measures discussed above.

Counterproductive behavior by employees poses a serious problem to organizations. The annual losses due to what is euphemistically termed *shrinkage*—that is, employee pilferage—is estimated to be in the billions of dollars. The use of illegal drugs and alcohol, absenteeism and tardiness, hostile acts, unauthorized computer usage, and sexual abuse in the workplace are equally important problems, although there are few reliable estimates of those costs. Over the past decade, a number of psychological tests to identify those job applicants who are most likely to engage in such counterproductive behavior have been developed.

Research has clearly shown that those tests of improper behavior that directly inquire about such behaviors, for example, "Have you ever stolen something of value from your employer?" produce more valid results than general personality measures. While such a finding may be counterintuitive, the research on these tests reveals that persons who score high on such indices typically justify their own behavior as less extreme than that of their peers. In other words, "Everybody does it and I do it less than the others!" The research on the usefulness of such measures of integrity and honesty has shown conclusively that, once such a program is initiated in an organization, there is a reduction in these counterproductive acts.

Readers may wonder why the several measures of creativity have not been included in this review. As we noted earlier in this chapter, these tests, which typically involve preferences for unusual responses as the measure of creativity, simply have not been shown to have utility in predicting creative behavior in the workplace. Further, scores on the openness to new experience scale on personality tests based on the five-factor approach to measurement also have shown little usefulness in this regard. One problem may be the difficulty in defining and measuring creativity in work situations.

Interviewing

While not strictly a measurement approach in that they rarely are standardized and almost never yield a quantitative score, interviews are included here, as they are the single most frequently used method for individual assessment, particularly for selection, and thus the interview is a critical component of the individual assessment process. While one could argue that our discussion of interviewing should appear elsewhere in this book, we strongly believe that it is most appropriate at this point.

Although the interview has been criticized for lack of reliability and validity, it can, if properly used, be a useful tool in the practice of individual assessment. Early reviews on the interview reported quite discouraging findings, leading to the conclusion that the interview was a poor selection tool. However, these findings were based on unstructured, vague interviews. More recent reviews (Campion, Palmer, & Campion, 1997; Campion, Purselsell, & Brown, 1988) conclude that the validity of the structured or behavioral interview is comparable to the paper-and-pencil tests discussed above. Moreover, the combination of test results and interview data significantly improve the validity of the assessment process as well as the recommendations that follow from that process.

Additional studies have conclusively shown that structured interviews are clearly superior to unstructured interviews; furthermore, structured interviews based on a formal review of the job, using a detailed job analysis to develop interview questions, are far superior to structured interviews without this rigorous job analysis base. In short, a planned, structured interview should be a valuable source of information in the individual assessment process. In addition, the interview provides flexibility to the interviewer, giving the interviewer the opportunity to probe, to follow up on vague information, and to obtain additional information to resolve inconsistencies in the candidate's profile. Other measures—such as the in-basket, job samples, and interactive exercises—also are available following the interview.

While information from these measures can add greatly to our knowledge about an individual, they are often difficult to administer and evaluate and, as a result, are used less often than paper-and-pencil tests and the interview.

Summary

Understanding the basic principles of measurement is crucial to choosing the must useful test(s) for the intended purpose, then using them effectively. These principles include (1) the normal distribution or bell-shaped curve, which has been shown over some three centuries to describe the expected distribution of a large number of scores or observations; (2) reliability, an indicator of the consistency and trustworthiness of a measure; (3) validity, or whether the test measures what it purports to measure; and (4) norms, which allow comparison of the score of an individual with those of a comparable set of individuals. Three categories of psychological tests—personality tests, specific job competency tests, and measures of cognitive ability—are described, together with a few other relevant types of tests that are few in number. An additional important assessment tool is the structured behavioral interview.

We also emphasize the role of the HR professional or assessor in establishing and maintaining the validity of the entire assessment process through his or her selection of assessment tools, oversight of their use to collect data, and interpretation of the data collected.

Finally, we have highlighted the fact that the research literature strongly supports the use of both measures of general cognitive ability and specialized aptitudes. Behaviorally based interviews provide another valid source of data for individual assessment. One point should clearly emerge from this chapter: there is potentially a large mass of valid information that can be gleaned from an individual assessment. The question then emerges as to how this information is collected and integrated into a meaningful picture of the individual, the topic of our next chapter.

Chapter Four

Collecting and Analyzing Assessment Data

The practice of individual assessment is best characterized as one of systematic and thorough data gathering, data analysis, and synthesis. Such assessments are conducted for the purpose of differentiating among qualified candidates for a single, unique position. The assessor's task is to acquire information about jobs and about people and then to analyze and synthesize what has been learned in order to recommend some form of employment action on the basis of the fit between the person being considered and the requirements of the job.

The practice of individual assessment is characterized by purposeful application of a variety of both standardized and informal methods and procedures to test this person/job fit. The sharing of the findings of any assessment is controlled by "a need to know," that is, in order to protect the privacy of the individual assessment data and recommendations, the findings should be made available only to those persons in the client organization who have a legitimate interest in those data and recommendations. This chapter describes the procedures of the individual assessment process in greater detail.

The person conducting the assessment may be either an employee of the organization, often a human resources specialist, or an outside consultant. The client, or end user, may request assessments only on an occasional or ad hoc basis, such as when a single job or job family opens, or periodically as different job vacancies occur. Some clients may also use the assessor for additional related services. For example, an assessor may be regarded as having special skill in evaluating people for financial service jobs or first-line manager positions and thus see only candidates for such positions. Or an assessor with skills in training and development may carry out such projects as well as assessment assignments. But regardless of the assessor's workflow, understanding the five steps involved in individual assessment is important.

Using the Five-Step Model of Individual Assessment

As we presented in Chapter Two, our process of individual assessment typically involves five, more-or-less discrete steps. These are (1) organization and work setting analysis; (2) job and person analysis; (3) integrating the job and person analyses; (4) reporting the results to the client; and (5) follow-up and program evaluation. After reviewing each step, we discuss how it should be used in the individual assessment process. See the figure on the next page.

Step 1. Organization and Work Setting Analysis

Basic information about the organization and work setting is collected to develop an understanding of these elements as a background for beginning the assessment. Any number of sources provide information about the organization and the work settings that it maintains, including the organization's annual report, its mission statement, some recent financial statements, formal statements of the organization's values and operating principles, any available results from employee attitude surveys, employee handbooks and those manuals used by the HR staff in the performance of their jobs, and any other readily available printed material about the organization.

Another tool that we have found useful as a source of information about the organization and its work settings is to ask a random sample of workers two simple questions. The first is, "If your best friend were coming to work here, what three specific bits of advice would you give that person about how to succeed here?" The second question is "What could your friend do early in working here

Model of the Individual Assessment Process

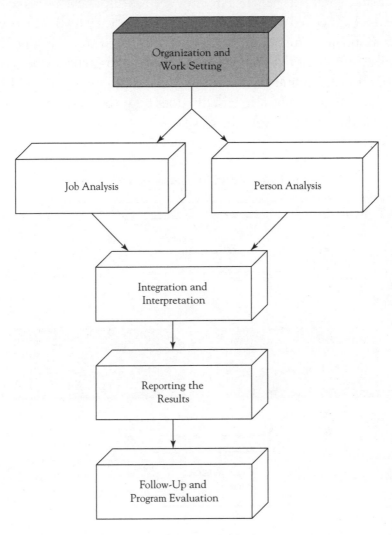

that would get that friend into serious trouble?" We have found that the answers to these questions provide a rich insight into the culture and operations of the organization, insights that the more formal documents simply do not reveal.

Unfortunately, there is no widely accepted method for understanding or describing an organization and its work settings. In this context, however, the focus should be clear. We are interested in learning about the manner in which the organization treats its human capital—its people. Are they seen as disposable resources to be used as needed and then discarded, or are they really the organization's most important assets, to be protected and developed? It is also important to know whether there is a discrepancy between what the organization states publicly about its employees and how it treats them and how it actually does treat them. In the current vernacular, do they "walk the talk"?

Model of the Individual Assessment Process

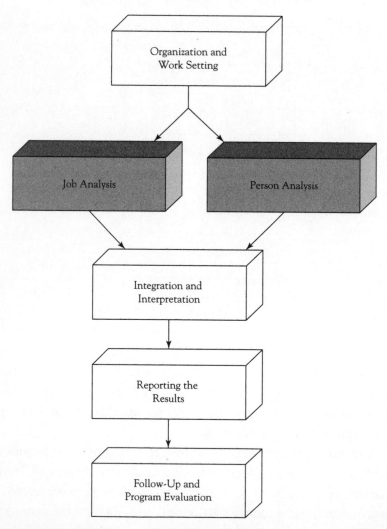

Step 2. Job and Person Analyses

A job analysis is performed to provide a detailed description of the target job, including the work activities involved and the competencies necessary to perform that job and their relative importance. These identified competencies form the basis for planning the next step, the person analysis. These competencies set the focus of the individual assessment, for it is essential to understand people as individuals with both strengths and weaknesses in the context of the job requirements of a specific job.

Job Analysis. A job analysis often begins with a careful study of the job description, which presumably should be available. Our experience has taught us that all too often no job description is available, or that what is available is out-of-date or incomplete. In any event, it is unlikely that the job description will do more than hint at the knowledge, skills, and abilities necessary to perform that job successfully—the major reason a job analysis is necessary. An example of a conventional narrative job description and competency specification is included in Appendix B, while Appendix C provides a more detailed, although brief, introduction to the job analysis process.

While there are a variety of approaches to performing a competent job analysis, they all share several features, including using multiple sources of information—incumbents, direct supervisors of the job, higher-level managers, and HR staff knowledgeable about the job—as well as observing the work actually being performed. Direct observation is especially important when the information from different sources is discrepant, for it may be the only way to resolve these discrepancies.

The process of job analysis should produce a set of job competency specifications, that is, a description of the work activities (WA) inherent in this specific job and an identification of the competencies, that is, the knowledge, skills, and abilities (KSAs), necessary to perform these activities successfully. An example of the model of competency specification at the entry level was presented earlier in Exhibit 2.1. Further examples of such competency specifications for first-line managers/supervisors and managers/executives can be found in Appendices D and E, respectively.

Our experience has shown us that the failure of the people involved to have a real understanding of what is required on a particular job is the most important cause of unsuccessful hiring and promotion decisions. A truly useful job analysis from a hiring or promotional point of view specifies the work competencies necessary for success in that specific job. A job competency is a behavior or set of behaviors—the knowledge, skills, and abilities necessary to accomplish a specific work task or achieve a specific goal. These competencies can range from the most simple, such as filing, operating a punch press, or answering callers politely and warmly, to the most complex, such as neurosurgery, getting along with a difficult supervisor, or doing a job analysis. The job analysis needs to determine with some degree of care the specific knowledge, skills, and abilities requirements of that particular job. Each specific job in an organization may require some unique technical competencies that need to be determined through a job analysis. Thus an administrative assistant position in one department may require knowledge and skill in making travel arrangements, whereas another department may require desktop publishing skills, in addition to those skills usually required for such positions. Only a thorough job analysis can distinguish and specify these requirements.

Person Analysis. It should be clear from the foregoing that the focus of the person analysis is to understand the person as an individual with both strengths and weaknesses in the context of the competencies required for success in a particular job. Obviously, as we move from simple entry-level assembly or clerical jobs through the first-line, managerial, and executive-level jobs, the scope of the person analysis broadens, making the task of individual assessment increasingly complex.

For entry-level jobs, individual assessments ordinarily involve a review of the job application plus (1) a brief measure of cognitive ability; (2) one or more appropriate tests of skills, such as clerical speed and accuracy or eye-hand coordination; (3) a measure of personality that focuses on the necessary personal-interpersonal skills such as conscientiousness or teamwork; and (4) a brief, focused behavioral interview to resolve any questions or inconsistencies uncovered in the earlier data collection. The goal of assessments at this level is determining the probability of success by this individual in this job.

Starting with the minimal qualifications presented in Exhibit 2.1 previously, as the level of job complexity and responsibility increases, the individual assessments necessary to evaluate candidates for these jobs also increase incrementally. These higher-level assessments require additional measures to be added to the assessment process to increase our understanding of the individual—always to answer the question of how well this person fits the job requirements specified by the job analysis. Typically such measures would include some tests provided in either a paper-and pencil or online version, such as a measure of general cognitive ability, of mechanical comprehension, of arithmetic ability, of personality characteristics, of integrity, and so on.

Another possibility would be including a small work sample, where the individual would be asked to actually demonstrate his or her skills in doing the job. Some routine jobs, like data entry clerk or forklift operator, readily lend themselves to such job sampling, while others do not. Again, the decision about what measures to include depends almost entirely on the job analysis; the person analysis is intended to determine the degree to which this person fits the template of success on a specific job in a specific organizational and work setting. Each incremental step in this process to obtain additional information about an individual must increase our understanding of this person in this job and, thus, enhance the accuracy of decision making.

Further along in this continuum of individual assessments, we find the use of increasingly complex and sophisticated measurement procedures and processes. For example, if the purpose of the assessment is the development of the individual, the procedure may include a self-assessment, the use of 360-degree feedback survey, and a more elaborate and detailed study of specific competencies, all designed to learn about the person's talents and potential for development in a specific organization.

At the executive level, there would be an in-depth study of the individual's resume; a battery of more complex psychological tests, such as critical thinking, cognitive complexity, and problem-solving ability; one or more personality tests that measure leadership, emotional stability, and other critical characteristics; and several lengthy behavioral interviews focused on the individual's work history, his or her successes and failures, and his or her role in each of these. At this level, the goal of assessment is to develop an in-depth understanding of the individual and the strengths and weaknesses that he or she would bring to this specific job.

Step 3. Integrating the Job and Person Analyses

The data about the job and its requirements and the data about the individual are then compared to determine the degree of fit between this individual and this job. The purpose of this process is to develop an understanding of this individual in the context of these job requirements. Once this level of understanding is attained, appropriate recommendations about employment decisions can be formulated for the client.

When hiring individuals for entry-level jobs, the recommendation often can be a simple one, to hire or not to hire, or a probability statement about the individual's likelihood of success on this job. For example, a simple clerical test might be administered to applicants for an entry-level position as a clerk. Any applicant scoring below the 50th percentile on the norms found in the test manual would simply be dropped from the applicant pool. There typically is little or no need for any additional integration or interpretation.

As the complexity of the job increases, however, so does the complexity of the decision making. Usually there is no single candidate who possesses the necessary level of skills in each important competency. Under such circumstances, the assessor needs to

Model of the Individual Assessment Process

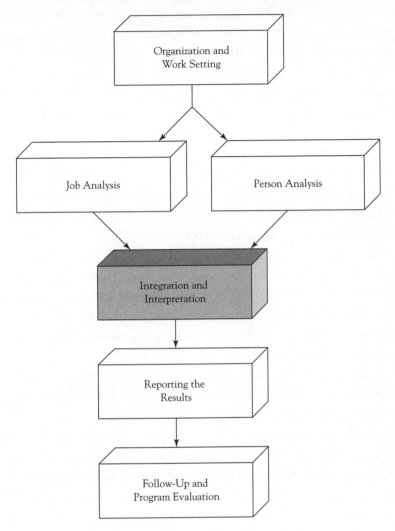

integrate and interpret the information about the candidate. The question often becomes "What are the tradeoffs that may be necessary to fill this job from this pool of candidates?"

Since we almost always find multiple candidates being considered, the analyses need to focus on the relative strengths and weaknesses of each of the individuals to meet the requirements of this particular job. Often it is possible to rank-order the candidates in terms of how likely they are to meet the demands of this job.

The answers to such questions of tradeoffs and ranking or ordering may be qualified or contingent on a non-linear weighting of the assessment data. For example, a weakness in one area may be compensated for by strength in another area. Recently, one of our clients in the office machine business needed to hire a sales representative to replace a highly assertive person with a strong bottom-line orientation. The successful candidate, a former schoolteacher, had a very different approach to the job, emphasizing a consultative sales style—one in which she focused on the customers' problems and worked collaboratively to find a feasible solution. Although the client initially had some reservations about hiring this person, she has been highly successful in the job, with the highest sales volume of any sales representative for several months.

Coming to such a recommendation involves an understanding of the idiosyncratic nature of human behavior. Such idiosyncrasy or individuality requires the assessor to attempt to understand the person holistically and make clinical judgments in integrating and interpreting the data rather than simply relying on test norms and quantitative findings.

This need for clinical judgments is intensified by the frequently encountered problem that there are no individuals with a good fit for the established template. This situation, however, does not change the client's need for an individual to fill this job. Thus the individual assessment task becomes one of identifying individuals who might be able to do the job if certain conditions are met—providing more than usual initial training or closer supervision, restructuring the job, and so on.

Clients expect that the individual assessment process will provide them with the data necessary to make an informed decision about the various applicants, which can produce a good bit of pressure on the assessor, particularly when none of the candidates seems genuinely suitable. Ethically the only course of action open to the assessor in such a quandary is to recommend that the client go back and begin the search process again or, at the very least, recognize that their only choice is far from an ideal one and be prepared to live with that choice.

Model of the Individual Assessment Process

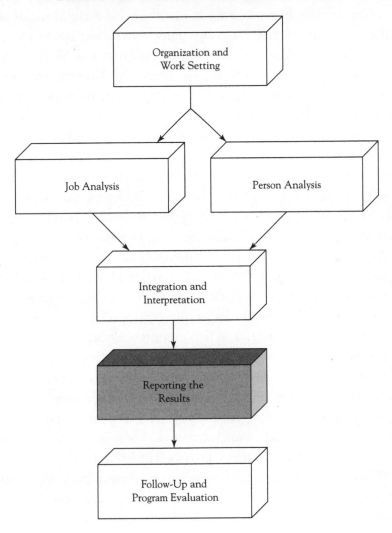

Step 4. Reporting the Results

Once the recommendations for middle- and upper-level positions are formalized, the assessor is responsible for reporting his or her recommendations to the client, together with sufficient data to justify the recommendations made. The client is always eager for this final report and will frequently press for its early release; at least this has been our experience. It is important not to give in to this pressure, particularly if more time is needed to fully comprehend and integrate the obtained data. Premature reporting can lead to an unfortunate situation if the final recommendations differ from those initially offered.

Although clients (internal and external) may request an immediate, brief oral report, for most assessments, and almost always for those prepared by external consultants, reporting involves a formal, written report. In preparing this written report, the assessor begins by developing a complete and detailed data set and then serves as the processor and interpreter of the data that have been generated, developing a composite characterization leading to a final recommendation. This approach is intended to produce a more thorough and integrated characterization of the individual than a mere analysis and description of individual assessment test results.

It is essential to note that, while there is a final recommendation, any report should also provide considerable additional data. In the report, each of the critical job skills or competencies ordinarily should be listed in order of importance to the job, followed by a rating of the individual on a five-point scale and an evaluation of the individual's strength and weakness on that competency, described in sufficient detail to ensure the client's understanding of the candidate in this specific area. Essentially, the ratings are a set of categories representing different degrees of demonstrated competence in the defined competency area. For this purpose, we recommend the rating definitions provided in Exhibit 4.1.

The impact of the organization's management philosophy and its culture must also be incorporated into whatever recommendations are offered. For example, a risk-taking organization with fluid boundaries will be more willing to accept a candidate who does not quite fit the template than would a more traditional, bureaucratic one. Failure to factor such cultural considerations into any recommendation reduces the probability that such recommendations will result in the desired actions.

Exhibit 4.1. Numerical Ratings of Competency

5   A rating at this level indicates mastery or almost complete mastery of this job skill or competence. An individual with a 5 rating would be considered an expert and a model for other employees and a special organizational resource.

4   A rating at this level represents advanced competency in this job skill or competence. At this level, the individual would be considered to have a journeyman-level of proficiency and would function independently and relatively unsupervised.

3   A rating at this level represents adequate competency in this job skill or competence. Adequate indicates sufficient skill to function with only occasional supervision or support.

2   A rating at this level indicates borderline or beginning job skill or competence. Some deficiencies in performance are expected, and an individual at this level requires fairly constant supervision and mentoring.

1   A rating at this level indicates little skill or competence in this job skill. Such an individual might be familiar with or have limited proficiency in this job skill. Generally, this level is adequate for employment only as a trainee where learning this skill is the only critical job requirement.

Finally, an initial, brief oral report plus a formal, written report does not obviate the need for a follow-up meeting that would include an oral review of the data, conclusions, and recommendations. This final oral report is an opportunity for the assessor to determine whether the information provided in the written report was sufficient to meet the client's needs and whether the client has any further questions or would like additional information about the candidate.

Model of the Individual Assessment Process

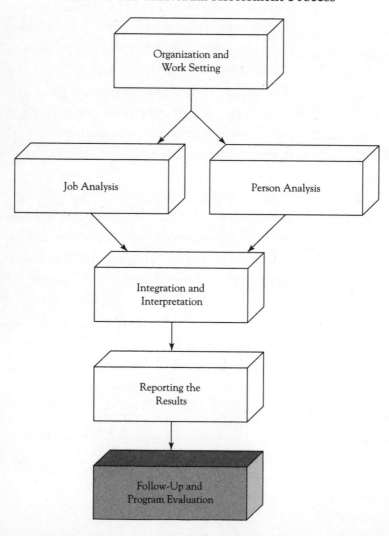

Step 5. Follow-Up and Program Evaluation

Finally, our approach to individual assessment is concerned with the long-term impact of our procedures on the operations of the client system. Has the introduction of our selection process actually improved the overall quality of the organization's selection process? Has employee turnover decreased? Has training time decreased? The answers to these and a myriad of other questions determine the degree to which we have been successful in improving the client's selection process.

In developing a process of program evaluation—assessing the consequences of installing a systemic process of individual assessment—particular attention should be paid to the concerns or problems that the client system identified in the first instance, namely, why were we asked to become involved in the selection process. Our experience is that if we can clearly identify the degree to which we have helped resolve these initial problems, we can conclude that our intervention was successful.

Because we recognize that clients often misidentify the underlying problem, part of the initial agreement should always include a provision for renegotiating it as we gather data about the client and how its various HR systems function. What has been identified as a selection problem may turn out to be a training problem or an equipment problem. But once we have renegotiated the identification of the problem, then we must assume responsibility for determining the degree to which we have resolved that problem to the client's satisfaction. It is important to recognize that we are not suggesting that satisfaction is based on good feelings, even though such feelings are important, but rather that it must be based on hard data.

The evidence that the systematic changes in individual assessment have produced systematic improvement in the way the client's HR systems function always should be the focus of follow-up and program evaluation. Furthermore, it is always worthwhile to gain an initial, in-depth understanding of the baseline data that the client system has available, as any changes will need to be tested against these baselines. For example, if the major issue is employee turnover, we need to know the turnover rate before our assessment process became part of the organization's standard operating procedures. Similarly, we would need to know the average training time and the drop-out and failure rates from training if training attrition was seen as the initial problem to be addressed. Without such baseline data, assessing the degree of improvement stemming from the new assessment program can only be impressionist and anecdotal. If follow-up or program evaluations are to be an integral part of a new assessment process, it is imperative to learn what data are readily available. The nature of the follow-up process that is proposed necessarily needs be based on the availability of baseline data.

Hard and Soft Data

The foundation of individual assessment is an understanding of individual differences, that is, the variability in human performance. Individual assessments involve two types of data—hard, those based on some formal measurement such as a psychological test, and soft, those based on the assessor's experience, intuition, and hunches. Soft data is often termed *clinical* or impressionistic data. The individual assessment process, however, often involves the combining of several bits of hard data, a process that tends to "soften" the data and, once these pieces of hard data are combined with the soft data in our efforts to achieve an in-depth understanding of an individual, the hard data have become quite soft. While the distinction between hard and soft data is an important one, the individual assessment process ordinarily requires an integration of the two in order to maximize the predictive power of the data. This integrative approach should produce a more thorough and accurate characterization of the individual.

Hard Data

We begin by noting that even hard data is not as hard as it might initially seem. While hard data is based on measurement by a standardized psychological test, different tests have different characteristics that determine its hardness. Some tests may be scored in absolute terms, while scoring for other tests is based on *ipsative* scoring procedures in which a high score on one scale is counterbalanced or offset by a low score on another scale. Also, absolute scores may have significantly different meanings, depending on the normative population used. For example, if we compare an entry-level applicant to the norms developed from experienced workers, we probably will come to a vastly different conclusion than if we use norms developed on entry-level applicants. Thus, it is essential that the norms used be appropriate for the target job. The more general the norms used, the softer the data becomes.

Many test manuals do not provide information on the spread of scores as a function of such demographics as age, race, gender, education, experience, training, and so forth. It is essential that test score manuals provide the distribution of test scores necessary to support interpretations so that appropriate conclusions may be drawn about individuals. When such demographic norms are available, it is essential that an appropriate norm group be chosen and that any conclusions drawn be firmly linked to the specific competencies required. The rigor used by the assessor in dealing with these issues will determine how hard the data being collected actually is.

As we discussed in Chapter Two, the manner in which the tests have been administered has an impact on the obtained results. For example, when a test of cognitive ability is taken on a computer, the obtained distribution of scores tends to be somewhat lower than that of scores obtained from the paper-and-pencil version of the same test. In other words, the average score from the computer version is usually lower than that from the traditional paper-and-pencil version, and this is especially true of timed tests. Thus, the appropriate norms are also a function of the mode of presentation, and the norms from one version usually will be inappropriate for the other version. In either case, it is essential that score distributions contained in the test manuals provide the necessary data to support interpretation of individual scores.

Interpretation of the hard data from a battery of tests needs to take into account the interaction of various test scores and other data. This interpretation and integration is individualized in that a single test score may have a different, unique meaning when viewed within a set of scores. Consider, for example, a candidate for a technical research position with a low score on a measure of caution or prudence. Coupled with high scores on a test of critical thinking, this low score would be interpreted quite positively, but it would not be seen in the same light when coupled with a low score on critical thinking. However, if the job vacancy were for a sales/marketing manager, this pattern of scores would have very different implications and probably would lead to a different recommendation. This is but one of the many dynamic interactions of test scores that lead to different outcome decisions. The point here is that test scores should not be interpreted in a vacuum, but require sophisticated judgments in order to be useful to the client.

In addition, test score interpretation must take into account the established validity data (Schmidt, Hunter, Croll, & McKenzie, 1983). Typically, higher scores indicate that the individual has more of a specific characteristic, and generally this is a positive sign for that individual. But that is not always the case; for example, a high score on caution is usually desirable in considering individuals for technical positions but may be undesirable for a sales position. Similarly, an individual may score too high on a cognitive ability test to be successful on a routine assembly job, especially long-term. It should be clear that the competencies required for job success set both the upper and lower limits of the competencies required for job success (McClelland, 1973).

In the individual assessment process, the interpretation of test score results and their meaning depends on the experience and the training of the assessor, which in turn impacts the quality of the entire assessment process. This interpretive process goes beyond simply reporting scores on testing results. It involves using these results as the basis for creating a portrait of the individual, illuminating his or her strengths and weaknesses in the context of a specific job. This process of creating that portrait requires the assessor to exercise a high level of skill and is critical to the quality of the process (Matarazzo, 1990). It is at this juncture that the hard data almost always tends to get soft.

Soft Data

While the initial focus of any assessment is usually on objective data, there is also the need to include soft or subjective data. Although objective measurement is absolutely essential, the soft, subjective, or clinical data are also important, as they often facilitate understanding of the hard test data to achieve an enhanced understanding of the individual. Among the several sources of soft data are the several observations of the person that can be recorded during the assessment process, a topic to which we return in Chapter Five.

In the process of collecting and analyzing the assessment data, questions about the candidate will inevitably emerge. The assessor needs to know as much about the candidate at the individual level as possible without moving into legally protected areas or becoming unnecessarily personal or intrusive. It is essential to ask questions of the candidate that illuminate his or her work style, motivation, job history, successes, and failures—factors that characterize the individual, as well as any other factors that may come into play to qualify our interpretation of the hard, objective data. Both hard and soft data are an important part of how we can best characterize the individual, and both require considerable care and caution in interpretation.

Assessment Procedures and Choices

We began our discussion of individual assessment by focusing on the job analysis for understanding of the job content and necessary competencies in order to decide how to go about developing a picture of the individual based on the individual assessment data. These data include the test scores and any other measurements that provide relevant information, most of which are developed in a very systematic way and can be used quantitatively for characterizing the individual. In integrating the data from these two sources—the job analysis and the person analysis—the objective is to assemble a single cohesive data set that allows the assessor to develop a portrait of an individual with reference to a specific array of competencies in a way that makes sense to the client, our ultimate customer. No recommendation should be developed or even considered until that descriptive formulation is firmly in mind.

Measurement Choices

Our approach of using test data as the foundation for individual assessments has considerable utility, for it offers the HR professional or psychologist the opportunity to make initial choices about testing strategy and procedures. To guide the reader, we have provided a listing of a representative sample of widely used, published tests in the major areas of individual assessment in Appendix I.

In practice, these professionals need to adapt and adjust the assessment process to a wide variety of conditions and circumstances, ranging from relatively simple to very complex. At the simplest level, measurement is focused on collecting objective data, usually limited in amount, that lead to decisions based on agreed-on rules, with minimal emphasis on interactive effects or interpretation of dynamic relationships. Only when contingencies exist or when the job exceeds a very basic level of complexity is there an opportunity or need for a more sophisticated approach to the assessment process, for example, when teamwork is required to do the job, when there are special requirements, or when the position to be filled is at an upper, or even middle, management level.

These increasingly sophisticated approaches, or procedures, are summarized in Exhibit 4.2 on page 74, examples selected to describe and differentiate different levels and areas of competency. By organizing them in a hierarchical fashion based on the level and complexity of required competencies, the assessor can develop a framework for choosing among multiple tests, then comparing and interpreting their scores for varied purposes. For example, for low-level jobs (entry-level supervisor or trainee), one set of tests would be employed; for a high-level position (executive level), different tests and different norms will be necessary. An important assessor competency is knowledge about the various tests, how each can best be used at the different levels, and the limitations of each. Without such knowledge, the quality of the assessment is compromised.

Learning About a New Test

One issue that frequently emerges is how one acquires knowledge and skill in using an unfamiliar test. We recommend the following steps:

1. Read the test manual thoroughly, especially that portion dealing with its development, validity, and norms.

2. Take the test yourself, using the administration instructions in the manual.

3. Estimate your performance on this test. How well do you think you did? What do you think the test will say about you?

4. Score the test and compare your predictions with your actual performance on the test.

5. If your predictions were on target, you have some insight into the test and how to interpret data from this test. If your predictions were way off the mark, consider the implications of this finding. Reread the manual and see whether you understand the author's rationale and how it should be applied. Remember, two possible conclusions exist: either your self-awareness may need to be recalibrated or the test may not be very valid. Until you resolve this dilemma, using this test is not a wise choice of assessment instruments.

6. Administering the test to several friends or colleagues whom you know well is still another step in learning about an instrument. Again, it is very useful to predict their scores based on your knowledge of them and then resolve any discrepancies, at least in your own mind.

Exhibit 4.2. Assessment Procedures at Different Levels of Job Complexity

Job Level	Assessment Procedures
Entry-Level Jobs	Only a minimum level of assessment for selection decision making is required. Test data are collected and handled statistically, and decision rules are specified. Normative data are relevant to the job and typically supported by evidence of content or criterion related validity.
Basic Clerical/ Office Jobs	Jobs at this level have both a range of complexity and a wide variety of specific competencies, ranging from simple data entry to complex administrative positions with career potential. Assessment involves psychometric and non-quantitative data and may include statistical and clinical integration, especially for higher-level jobs.
Professional and Administrative Jobs	Jobs at this level involve a broad variety of competencies and a range of complexity with career potential. Jobs are usually non-supervisory but often do include leadership roles. There is a strong emphasis on a high level of expertise. Assessments include collection of both quantitative and clinical data and complex analyses of these data.
Production Jobs	Jobs in this category demand a variety of competencies, but with an emphasis on dealing with things and ideas, usually in the physical world. The jobs, often in the skilled trades and crafts, often require specialized knowledge about tools, processes, and materials, but not high educational achievement.

Job Level	Assessment Procedures
Sales and Customer Relations Jobs	Jobs in this category involve a wide range of complexity but a narrow range of competencies. These jobs emphasize competency in dealing with both people and ideas. The assessment includes collection of both quantitative and clinical data and complex analysis of these data.
Technical and Analytical Jobs	Jobs in this category are generally at the higher level of complexity and emphasize content involving ideas and, to a lesser extent, people. Data sources are quantitative and clinical and are analyzed with lesser emphasis on interpretation of subtle facets.
Supervisor and Entry-Level Management Jobs	Jobs in this category are average in terms of complexity and represent a broad range of competencies, especially in dealing with people and in problem solving. The assessment includes collection of both quantitative and clinical data and complex analysis of these data.
Middle- and Executive-Management Jobs	The spectrum of required competencies is extremely broad with a high degree of complexity and covers most managerial work with a strong emphasis on people skills. The assessment includes collection of complex quantitative and clinical data and high-level analyses of these data.

What should be clear from the above is that it is possible to learn about an instrument on one's own. However, it does require time and effort. But as new and apparently useful tests come into the market, it is important to learn about them and test their usefulness from a personal point of view. Despite the validity data, which may or may not be contained in the manual, unless we understand the test on a very personal basis, we are unlikely to use it effectively in assessing others.

Choosing Tests

In developing the requirements and procedures for conducting individual assessments, we have based our work on the premise that there is no one, single, optimal way of developing a data set. Individual assessment is the process of individualized evaluation of the characteristics of a particular individual. This does not mean, however, that the process is random measurement. The research data, as well as our own experience, indicate that the overall validity of the individual assessment process is a function of the unique or *idiosyncratic* work of the practitioner, that is, the practitioner's understanding of the job and organization requirements on the one hand and skill and experience on conducting assessments on the other (Ryan & Sackett, 1987).

The most important consideration in selecting a battery of tests for assessing candidates for a particular job is the list of competency specifications—the target-job requirements—developed through the job analysis. In other words, tests should be selected that can assess a person's degree of competence in each of the areas that have been identified in the competence specification resulting from the job analysis. It also provides a strong line of defense against a legal charge of discriminatory hiring. As an example, in an entry-level competencies specification for an assembly job, five different competencies are identified as necessary for success: the ability to (a) work effectively with others; (b) learn new materials; (c) perform basic arithmetic functions; (d) solve basic physical work-related problems; and (e) follow instructions and direction. In addition, each of these competencies is rated on importance to success on the job, using a five-point scale.

In selecting a test battery for this specific entry-level job, we would include (a) a teamwork scale; (b) a brief measure of cognitive ability; (c) a test of basic arithmetic skills; (d) a mechanical comprehension test; and (e) a measure of verbal comprehension. Each of these measures is presumably functionally related to the competency identified by the same letter. Which specific test is used will depend on a variety of factors, including the "importance" rating of the competency, the relative validity of the several available measures, the appropriateness of the available norms, ease of scoring, cost, availability, the assessor's familiarity with an instrument, and a variety of other, even more idiosyncratic considerations. For those competencies rated as highly important (ratings of "5" or "4" on the five-point scale), we might choose to use a longer, more costly in both administrative time and dollar cost measure or we might use multiple measures; we are less likely to exercise these options for competencies rated as less important ("1" or "2").

The competencies specification also helps set the content of the behavioral-based interview. In our example of the entry-level assembly job, we would ask the individual such questions as, "Tell me about a time when you found it hard to get along with another, difficult co-worker. How did you handle the situation?" Or "Give me an example of a time when you were unsure of what to do in a work situation. Explain the situation and how you handled it." With some competencies, the interview may be a better measure of the competence than a test. In the prior example of the entry-level assembly job, the willingness to follow direction can be readily ascertained by the interview, precluding the need for a test of that competence. It should be clear from this example that the competencies specification really drives the test selection, the interview, and the entire individual assessment process.

In conducting individual assessments, moreover, different assessors may use different tests and other approaches to create the basic data set. Different tests may yield somewhat different results because they are based on different theoretical models of human behavior, because they have different emphases or measure different characteristics, or even because they are formatted somewhat differently. Nevertheless, two different assessors using similar but unique sets of measures should still arrive at very similar conclusions when both are focusing on the same job and set of required competencies. When this does not occur, alarm bells about the validity of the assessment process should be ringing.

As noted earlier, as we progress through increasingly specialized or higher-level jobs, higher levels of skill are required of the assessor. A comparison of the competency model for entry-level jobs in Exhibit 2.1 with those for supervisory/first-line management in Appendix D and senior-management/executive level in Appendix E makes these differences quite apparent.

As the complexity of the data increases, so do the issues involved in analyzing and understanding these data. The movement from relatively objective measurement and clear-cut decision rules to ever-more-subjective data and idiosyncratic decision making dramatically increases the need for sophisticated assessor skills.

Benchmarking

Another approach to identifying the necessary competencies—both technical and personal/interpersonal—for a specific job and how they best can be measured is through *benchmarking*. Benchmarking is the process whereby the competencies necessary for job success are determined by comparing the results of individual assessments of a sample of successful incumbents on a specific job with those from a sample of poor or mediocre performers on that job. The differences in the pattern of results between the two groups can then be used as a benchmark against which to compare applicants for that job.

Benchmarking can help an organization to better understand the requirements that make for job success. Moreover, it is arguably the most common method of establishing the validity of an assessment process. Despite not being generally understood as such, benchmarking clearly identifies those characteristics associated with success on a particular job and thus is *criterion related*, that is, where test scores have been shown to be statistically related to an important aspect of job success. This form of criterion relatedness is the essential determinant of whether or not using an assessment instrument is legitimate.

Conducting a Benchmark. Benchmarking is a particularly useful tool in establishing both the personal/interpersonal characteristics and the level of cognitive ability associated with success on a specific job. Using benchmarks to set these parameters in individual assessments provides objective data about these critical characteristics, which eliminates the guesswork and speculation about what is necessary for success.

Developing the benchmark for a specific job involves the following specific steps:

1. Conduct a job analysis by asking a panel of persons knowledgeable about a job to identify independently the knowledge, skills, and abilities each of them assumes to be important for success on the job. This group may involve incumbents, first-line supervisors, managers, and any others with knowledge of that job. This information can be collected through interviews, questionnaires, or e-mail.

2. Analyze the content of the job analysis to identify the level of knowledge, skills, and abilities required, as described in Appendix C, Introduction to Job Analysis. This analysis should identify those KSAs that are most critical to success on the job—ratings of 4 or 5. These data provide the foundation for benchmarking.

3. Identify the measures, including tests, that can best measure those most critical KSAs. Appendix I provides a list of tests that we have found useful for that purpose.

4. Identify two groups of incumbents: one group should be composed of individuals who are top performers on the job and the other group of poor or mediocre performers. How these groups have been composed, of course, should not be revealed to those chosen. In some organizations there will be strong objections to identifying any current employee as poor or mediocre. Under such circumstances, it is appropriate to ask for an identification of low average or average performers, which is often less problematic. It is important that, in order to avoid bias and favoritism, job success be clearly identified by objective performance criteria, such as dollar value of sales, amount of rework, absenteeism, disciplinary actions, and the like.

5. Administer the several different tests, each tapping a different function or attribute identified by the panel as important for job success, to all those individuals in the two groups. Those tested should simply be told that the testing is part of an effort by management to better understand the factors involved in success on that job, which, in fact, it is.

6. The two sets of data—one from the top performers and the second from the average or poor performers—should be examined to determine which of the test scores most clearly differentiated the most successful incumbents from the least.

7. The obtained pattern of differences then can be used as a template for selecting new employees.

While a job analysis plays a vitally important role in determining the competencies required for job success, it is often difficult to know which psychological tests are likely to provide valid measures of these competencies. This is especially true of personal/interpersonal characteristics and cognitive ability. The inferential leap from the KSAs of a job analysis to the characteristics identified by psychological measurement requires a level of expertise rarely possessed by line managers. But identifying these characteristics through testing is necessary to identify those who will succeed on the job. As a result, in order to make certain such factors are included, we almost always include a broad measure of personality and a brief test of cognitive ability in all benchmarking studies. Even at the entry level, when the job is critical to the organization, they are necessary and should always be included.

A Case Example. The results of such a benchmarking process often yield surprising results. In a recent application of this methodology to the sales force at a large producer of envelopes, the largest difference between the two groups was on cognitive ability, with the most successful sales people having considerably higher scores. Up to this point the sales force had been selected on the basis of extroversion—the capacity to successfully engage others in social interactions and be resilient to rejection. While extroversion scores were high for both groups, there was only a slight difference in the means.

On examination, the explanation of why this had occurred became very obvious. Most of the company's customers were financial service institutions and, in "the old days," they were mostly small-town banks in which the purchasing decisions were made by the presidents—usually after a round of golf. But with the consolidation of the banking industry and the increasing importance of automation, the purchasing decisions were now being made by the director of information technology, so a successful sale required a good bit of knowledge and problem-solving skills—exactly what is measured by tests of cognitive ability. The old sales process no longer worked, and the selection for the new sales process required a different set of skills, which clearly was revealed by benchmarking.

Additional Reasons for Benchmarking. This case example illustrates one of the important benefits of using benchmarking, namely, it provides management with information about the nature of a specific job and the competencies necessary to do that job successfully. This is often new information and can be helpful to management in identifying reasons for generally poor performance, that is, limitations in their present workforce.

As we began this section, we noted that benchmarking is a form of validation. Benchmarking is a criterion-based process for evaluating the validity of a battery of psychological tests—a form of *concurrent validity* that was discussed in greater detail in Chapter Three. At this point we do need to note that the results of benchmarking should provide evidence of the validity of the assessment process in the face of legal challenges, an important consideration in this litigious age.

Limitations of Benchmarking. Benchmarking often causes managers problems, as they have relatively fixed ideas about what makes for a good employee and resist giving up their ideas. In the case cited above, the vice president of sales was very reluctant to accept the results of our benchmark. He was convinced that he knew exactly who would make good sales representatives for the company—people exactly like him! It took some convincing for him to accept the results of the benchmark and recognize that "the times are a changin'." Before instituting a benchmarking process, it must be recognized that all too often the facts do not speak for themselves and that the assessors may have a fight on their hands in order to have their recommendations adopted.

A different issue is that benchmarking identifies the competencies necessary for success today and not tomorrow; that is, benchmarking does not take into account future job requirements. Thus, benchmarking involves planning through the rear-view mirror. How to include future requirements that obviate this concern is addressed in Chapter Six.

Reporting and Follow-Up Choices

Once having reached the point of understanding how well the individual meets the competency specifications of the specific job, the assessor is responsible for reporting the results of the assessment. Developing the report to the client presents a final opportunity to reconsider the tradeoffs between the individual's relative strengths and weaknesses with respect to the job and how these factors should impact the final recommendation. When multiple candidates are being evaluated, drafting the report may require a detailed comparison of the relative strengths and weaknesses of the several individuals and how these relative differences may impact future job success. Nevertheless, each evaluation must stand on its own merits. However, as we will see in Chapter Five, it is always the responsibility of the end user to make the final choice among the several candidates, as only the end user can evaluate the relative costs and benefits of choosing one of these individuals to fill this particular job.

In drafting the report, it is also necessary to maintain a continuous awareness of the normative characteristics and the validity, or relative predictive value, of the obtained test scores. Our approach to assessment provides a significant opportunity for organizations to conduct validity studies that have the potential for enhancing the value of an organization's human resources management as well as providing a strong defense against charges of discriminatory hiring practices.

Summary

We have described how to implement our five-step approach for conducting, integrating, and reporting individual assessments used for employment purposes. It links a multiple-measure approach to individual assessment, using both hard and soft data, to a set of competency specifications derived from a specific job analysis. We tacitly acknowledge the complexity of both data sets—one describing the individual and the other the job. Linking the two to develop a detailed picture of how a specific individual would be expected to function in a specific job and reporting the data and conclusions in a coherent and useful report that enables the client to resolve an employment problem completes the process.

It is important for assessors to learn about tests with which they are not familiar; a standard process for doing this is suggested.

Selecting appropriate objective measures of the individual and combining them with suitable soft data, conducting a comprehensive job analysis, and interpreting the data require the HR professional or psychologist to act as data processor as well as collector. It is a true test of the assessor's knowledge, skill, and judgment. We also discuss the role of benchmarking and how to conduct a benchmark, which can be used both as a template for selecting new employees and to establish the validity of the assessment process. Some advantages and some limitations of the benchmarking process are also identified. The consequence of doing all this, however, is a useful report, one that answers the end user's questions and helps lead to a useful decision. Such reports, however, require the assessor to develop and integrate a complex set of data, which is the focus of the next chapter.

Chapter Five

Developing and Integrating Individual Assessment Data

A substantial amount of information is usually generated from the individual assessment practice. It is important that the volume of data not overwhelm the assessor. The optimal strategy to avoid being overwhelmed is to keep the goal of the assessment process in mind—to understand the individual and to link this understanding of the person to the target job for which the assessment was conducted. The result of this linkage—the job/person match—should serve as a compass guiding the way to integrating the available data.

The individual assessment process involves collecting information from a variety of sources to develop a picture of the whole individual. This picture always must be in terms of identifying the job-related competencies previously identified as important for success in this job. Thus the task now is to develop a composite picture of the person based on information obtained from:

- Résumé, including data on education, training, and prior experience;
- Interview data;
- Psychological tests, including measures of personality, specific job competencies, cognitive ability, management and leadership, and honesty/integrity;
- Analysis and evaluation of content of any work product or portfolio provided;
- Job samples; and
- Observed behavior.

Choosing Measures

The foundation of any individual assessment depends on the validity of measures used, their psychometric properties. The intent of any individual assessment process is to develop and present valid data in a format that is useful to the end user(s) in the workplace. The research evidence, together with our many years of practical experience, have proven to us that a competent assessor can examine and analyze the data accumulated about an individual and accurately predict how well that person would perform on a specific job. These linkages between the assessment data and the job criteria are derived by application of the empirical validation research findings, as detailed in the previous chapter, and the prior experience of the assessor. It is possible to use measures based on content, predictive, or construct validity or simply to use a solid track record of experience as the strategic basis of an individual assessment. However, both the choice of strategy and its implementation should always be based on the extensive experience of individual assessment practitioners who have the opportunity to observe individuals in the assessment setting and, later, in the work setting (Prien, Schippmann, & Prien, 2003).

The following example is an illustration of how both the research literature and assessor experience can be blended in making a prediction of success. While it is clear that low scores on a mechanical comprehension test are strongly suggestive that individuals with such low scores will not learn readily how to perform on an assembly job, these low scores can be compensated for by high scores on measures of the personality trait of conscientiousness. In other words, such persons will try harder to learn the task and thus increase their chances of success. Understanding that high conscientiousness can compensate, at least to some degree, for low mechanical comprehension is an example of how blending research and experience lies at the core of the individual assessment process.

This example highlights the importance of the assessor's knowledge and skill in interpreting test data on the individual level, an issue we initially raised in Chapter Two. Drawing inferences about the characteristics of a person based on the results of a battery of tests requires an understanding of the degree of validity of each of the tests employed, the appropriateness of the norms used, and a variety of personal factors, including fatigue, unwillingness or inability to be candid, language, or cultural disconnects, among many others. But as Meyer, Finn, Eyde, Kay, Moreland, Dies, Eisman, Kubiszyn, and Reed (2001) make clear in their comprehensive analysis of the research literature, psychological tests provide useful data about people that is not conveniently available from other sources. As is the case with medical tests such as X-rays and analyses of blood chemistry, it is the expertise of the assessor that allows these data points to be transformed into information, that is, a meaningful and accurate description of the person and his or her current level of functioning.

In choosing a series of tests to use in an assessment process, there are three general rules to follow: (1) test for more than a single competency (even the simplest jobs involve multiple skills); (2) use more than one test to measure the most critical competencies in order to provide solid, valid data; and (3) use different approaches to measuring these critical competencies in order to give the person maximum opportunity to demonstrate the competence. Thus one might use both a paper-and-pencil test of mechanical comprehension and a measure of manual dexterity involving assembling small objects. It is through the use of such a multi-measure approach that we increase both the reliability and validity of our recommendations, making them more useful both for those we are assessing and for the end user.

Just as each practitioner chooses a strategy for each assessment process, so will each prefer certain instruments to others. That is, each has his or her own favorites. Ours are listed in Appendix I. There are, of course, thousands of different tests and measures commercially available that assessment practitioners can use. Some of these measures are commonly used, while others are less well known, and still others are custom developed measures. The standard for using a measure is that every test used should have a reasonable degree of validity evidence to support its application in a specific individual assessment process.

The Database

Integrating the observations from a diverse set of sources is often a challenging task, one that may seem undoable, especially to the novice. Let us examine each of these data sources for suggestions about how they might contribute to integration.

Résumés

In our experience, we have found it is important to begin the integration process with a careful review of the résumé. The résumé provides an overview of the individual's life as he or she prefers to have it seen and understood. It also provides a framework for the interview, which should always be based on an analysis of the résumé.

The review of the résumé should always involve a focus on two elements: first, an examination of the dates involved in the person's history, especially for any unexplained gaps or discrepancies that need to be explored, and second, for developing the questions for a behavioral interview. "What led you to switch jobs from ABC to XYZ?" "Tell me how you went about making these changes in the sales group." "Give me an example of when you tried to discipline a subordinate and it just didn't work out." Such questions always should be based on the résumé review and help an assessor more completely understand the individual's approach to work and the workplace. Indeed, the care with which the résumé has been completed is itself a useful source of data about the person.

The increased use of the Internet for transmitting résumés in response to a position posting on a *job board,* that is, a computer-based listing of a job vacancy, has resulted in most employers receiving an immediate flood of résumés after the posting. These résumés have been sent automatically through a matching of key words in the résumé with elements of the job posting. Most employers then use a computer-based screening tool to sort the résumés. For example, only résumés that list five or more years of experience in a specified field would actually be reviewed and those with less experience rejected. Further, there are now several job boards that ask those applicants whose résumés pass through this initial screen to complete a short battery of psychological tests that typically include a measure of cognitive ability and a measure of personality. These changes as a function of the ever-increasing use of the Internet are clearly impacting the practice of individual assessment, probably not for the better, as there is no human assessor who brings his or her expertise into the process.

Many résumés, particularly at the professional level, include a self-reported list of previous accomplishments, both on the job and in other activities, including community service. Such a listing can be seen as a highly relevant, behaviorally based report of competencies. Research (for example, Hough, 1984) has shown that analyses of these listings can provide reliable indices of important job-related competencies that might otherwise not be identifiable. As we noted above, these listings also can provide the basis for a series of questions, the answers to which will further illuminate this individual's pattern of competencies.

It is important, however, to recognize that many résumés contain less than truthful information. One study of résumés reported that almost one-third of all the information in résumés was inaccurate. Included were inflated titles, inaccurate dates to conceal gaps in employment or "job hopping," exaggerations of educational credentials, including incomplete and mail-order degrees, inflated salaries and bonuses, exaggerated accomplishments, and outright lies about duties and accomplishments. While many of these can only be identified by a careful background check (which we strongly advocate as part of the hiring process), the interviewer has an opportunity to do considerable checking through the behavioral interview, our next topic.

The Interview

Interviewing the individual provides two types of data about that person. Obviously the purpose of an assessment interview, especially a behavioral interview as carefully described by Latham and Sarri (1984), is to gather more information about that person—about how he or she sees him- or herself, his or her education and training, job history, the accomplishments and obstacles encountered, and so on. The interview, however, provides additional data about the individual. The interview is a behavioral sample of how this person interacts. How appropriately is the person dressed for the interview? While a tank top, torn jeans, and flip-flops may be appropriate for some situations, it is not appropriate attire for an employment interview. Dressing for success usually starts with the interview!

We previously noted that a proper assessment interview is always based on a careful review of the résumé. It is never a casual conversation about trivia. If the interviewee deflects behavioral questions about information contained in the résumé, it should always serve as a warning sign about the truth of the résumé information. While it is usually inappropriate to confront the person about such signs of deceit, they should be noted, and the need for a thorough background check becomes urgent.

We strongly suggest that the interview be conducted *before* the psychological tests are scored and analyzed. A psychological test profile carries considerable weight in the individual assessment process. Viewing the results of such tests before the interview involves a serious risk that the interview process will be contaminated by such knowledge. In such circumstances the interview can become biased, an example of the "Pygmalion effect." However, reviewing the testing first allows you to explore discrepancies in the test results, or to ask follow-up questions on an admission of counterproductive behavior on an honesty/integrity test, or just to explore a sense that the candidate has not been adequately forthcoming. But these issues can also be addressed in a second interview specifically designed for the purpose of follow-up that avoids the risk of initial contamination.

It is important to recognize that the structure of the interview—the focusing on behaviors—is an important element in determining its usefulness. A job interview is never a casual conversation; rather, it is an organized effort to get to know and understand the interviewee, his or her strengths and weaknesses, and how well that pattern fits the job requirements. The interview requires careful preparation, including a study of the materials at hand. For example, there now is an opportunity to make inquiries about time gaps in the résumé.

There is ample evidence (for example, Campion, Palmer, & Campion, 1997; Campion, Pursell, & Brown, 1988) to support the conclusion that only a structured behavioral interview can provide valid information that adds to the individual assessment process. Such an interview is a planned, purposeful process aimed at further identifying the specific strengths and weaknesses of this individual and, as such, requires forethought, preparation, and planning.

Psychological Tests

As we noted earlier, the tests used in an individual assessment should be chosen because they tap characteristics important for success on a particular job. In the best of all worlds, we would have strong empirical data to support the use of each test used, that is, validity studies in this organization would have shown that this test is significantly correlated with success in this job. But this is rarely the case. Rather, appropriately selected tests in general are related to success in jobs of this type in a variety of employment settings and thus are useful for selection.

We should approach each assessment with a clear understanding of what a strong candidate would look like from a psychological testing point of view. Then, in reviewing our test findings, we should focus on the question of how well this person's test scores fit this pattern of an ideal candidate for this position. Low scores on a test are not necessarily "bad" scores, nor are high scores necessarily "good" scores. The question always is "How well does this individual fit the ideal pattern?" This question can never be answered "yes" or "no," but rather is always a question of degree. The five-point rating scale presented in Chapter Four can be used to identify the perceived degree of fit in each case, and then these ratings can be used in comparing candidates when such a comparison is required.

A number of cautions should be observed in reviewing psychological test results. Any extreme score, that is, any score at the extremes of the distribution, top and bottom 2 percent, raises a question. These questions include the appropriateness of this particular test for this person, the possibility of coaching on the test, inappropriate prior knowledge, practice effects, and so on. Another question that always needs to be kept in mind is whether an appropriate norm group was used to profile the test, an issue we explored in Chapter Three. This is especially important when using computer-based tests, as discussed earlier in Chapter Two.

On personality and honesty/integrity tests the question of faking is always at issue. While we know that so-called "obvious" items produce more valid measures of personality than do "subtle or covert" items, these are also the items that are most susceptible to faking. Most tests of personality do include some measure of faking or attempting to make a good impression. These items include behaviors that are socially acceptable but highly unlikely to be true. For example, "I have never told a lie, even to spare the feelings of a friend." While we may wish that to be true, it is a highly unlikely behavior. Thus, high scores on a social desirability or good impression scale raise a warning sign about the tendency of the test taker to have tried to present an overly positive view of himself or herself.

When results from more than one test are available, the similarities and differences among the scores need to be examined. Within the limits of the reliabilities of the several tests, the data ought to converge into a comprehensible picture, or the results need to be reexamined. Finally, after our review of the résumé and completing the interview, we usually have a tentative view of the individual, his or her cognitive level, the degree of extroversion and other underlying personality traits, skills level, and so on. Then when we review the psychological test results, we need to be aware of the degree to which our expectations have been met. When they are met, in other words, when the psychological tests confirm our initial impressions, we can conclude that we are on relatively safe ground and that we are on the right track in developing the required picture of the person. On the other hand, when our impressions are not confirmed, we need to carefully examine the discrepancies and attempt to determine, as best we can, the reasons for this lack of alignment. We should not proceed further in developing our interpretation of our data until this matter is laid to rest.

Work Products

In many occupations, such as artist, writer, graphic designer, architect, and some types of engineering, a portfolio of work products that represent samples of the person's work is often available (Reilly & Chao, 1982). Such a portfolio can provide considerable insight into the competencies of the individual who produced the portfolio. But most of us who practice assessment usually are not sufficiently knowledgeable to evaluate the quality of such work products or portfolios. In these cases, we need to ask the individual to leave the portfolio for expert review. This is often problematic, as the person will be extremely reluctant to allow such precious material to leave his or her possession. In such cases, setting up a return visit with the portfolio when an appropriate expert is available may be the only alternative.

One problem with using such work products is that they may not actually be the work of the person involved. In one such case, an applicant for an academic position provided a set of reprints of journal articles altered to show himself as the author. Unfortunately for the candidate, this was an area in which we had done some research and we quickly recognized a clever forgery. If this had not been the case, however, this charming psychopath would have had the job! Again, the need for careful checking is apparent.

Work Samples

Asking an individual to demonstrate the required competencies in real time is another way of collecting important data. Many lower-level, specific competencies are best assessed through work samples, such as data entry, operating a fork lift, or drafting an e-mail response to a customer complaint, but these measures often require the availability of equipment, which is not always possible.

For higher-level jobs, there are two major types of work samples: one is the in-basket test for managers (Schippmann, Prien, & Katz, 1990) and the other is interactive role plays involving many supposed real-life situations. The in-basket test, of which there are many versions, typically asks the individual to assume that he or she is taking the place of a manager who has been suddenly incapacitated. The individual is then given a variety of memos, reports, telephone messages, and e-mails directed to the absentee manager that are to be arranged in priority order for action. The resulting list is then evaluated as a test of the individual's problem-solving approach. The research on the value of the in-basket procedure suggests that it is of limited benefit despite its wide usage (Schippmann, Prien, & Katz, 1990).

Role plays are another approach to assessing higher-level performance. Here the assessor provides a description of a situation that the individual may confront in the job and then asks the individual to respond to that situation as he or she would actually respond to such a situation. The assessor or an accomplice plays the role of another person involved in that situation, with the assessor becoming the observer. For example, an applicant for a sales manager's position may be asked to deal with a sales representative whose performance is substandard but who has been distracted by family problems. How skillful is the person in dealing with the problem? Is there an awareness of both the personal and organizational issues involved, and so on? While such role plays provide interesting insights into the behavior of the individual, the lack of standardization and normative data limit their usefulness.

Observed Behavior

Although the individual assessment situation is not a realistic work situation, it does provide the assessor with an opportunity to observe the individual responding to the overall assessment process. These opportunities include meeting the receptionist, entering the testing situation, responding to the interview, having lunch, and so on. While such unobtrusive observations may be partially obscured by the anxiety many persons experience when being evaluated, such observations need to be included in the development of a comprehensive picture of the individual.

These observations begin with the entry of the individual into the evaluation situation. How does the person introduce himself or herself? What is his or her response to any waiting time? As we noted before, how appropriately is the person dressed? How attentive is he or she to the testing instructions? How many questions about the testing are raised and in what manner? How straightforward do the answers to the interview questions seem? How much does the person press for feedback about the evaluation process? These are just some of the myriad of observations than can be made during the assessment process by any number of others.

In developing an individual assessment process, it is always important to remember that there are multiple opportunities to observe the person in a variety of situations. The assessor must plan a procedure that systematically records these observations, either on a simple record form or in a computer database, and makes them available for later analysis. These need not be lengthy, interpretative comments, just records of direct observations. From these many observations from a variety of sources and different observers, we look for consistencies in the behaviors, consistencies that give us clues about the type of person we are evaluating. These are the clues that we then need to integrate with the other data points that we have collected.

Processing the Database

Once we have completed the database, we are faced with the task of integrating what is at best a myriad of detail and, all-too-often, bits of contradictory data. For example, how do we account for the fact that this senior financial analyst with an earned MBA earns an IQ score of only 106 on a well-standardized measure of intellect? Organizing and integrating the information that we have generated in the initial step of the individual assessment process is usually a daunting task. It becomes easier, however, once we review how we arrived at this stage of the assessment process and the steps that we now need to follow. After collecting information about the individual from a variety of sources, the next steps are to:

1. Analyze and evaluate this information to identify the critical characteristics of the individual and his or her performance;
2. Make inferences about how the observed behavior and performance may impact job success;
3. Place values on these inferences in terms of potential success on the job and acceptance in the organization; and
4. Draw conclusions and make recommendations.

Thus, the procedure is to *describe, analyze and evaluate, draw inferences, place values on these inferences and their potential impact on performance,* and, finally, *draw conclusions.*

Analyzing and Evaluating the Data

In analyzing and evaluating data, we focus on the data at hand and its consistency. Do we think that we can trust our results? Are there still unanswered questions that require additional data collection?

Do we have sufficient data to begin to draw inferences about this person that will have important real-life implications? Can we develop a convincing presentation that will really answer our end user's questions? Only when we can answer these questions in the affirmative should we move ahead to the next step, the drawing of inferences.

In reviewing the extensive database usually collected in an individual assessment, any unexpected or discrepant data will command immediate attention—data that clearly did not meet our expectations. These are the expectations, both implicit and explicit, that we developed during our interchanges with the individual. As we asked in an earlier section on observations, "What impression did the individual make on us and how does that fit with the rest of the data?" For example, Jane, an apparently open and friendly applicant for an executive assistant position, shows clear signs of low tolerance for stress and suspiciousness toward people. How do we reconcile these two bits of discrepant data? While we may not be able to do so immediately, we identify this as an issue to resolve by further analysis of the data.

It is important to remember in conducting an analysis to continually use the specific job analysis as the template through which to view the person under scrutiny. Jane may very well be open and friendly in casual meetings but a fierce protector of the executive inner sanctum, exactly what is required to be successful in this job.

Although a person's first reaction to the unexpected is usually significant and natural, the more important part of the analysis is the identification of how the pattern of the various strengths and weaknesses of the individual would meet the demands that have been identified in the job analysis. Once this pattern of strengths and weaknesses has been clearly identified and the issues implicit in the unexpected have been noted, we can turn to drawing the inferences about the individual's potential for success in the job.

The current widespread use of computer-based interpretations of test results raises an important issue. These computer-generated test interpretations are generic and not necessarily related to a specific job. It is clear that interpretations based on the benchmarking of this particular job are far more likely to provide valid results.

Finally, it is worth noting that not all data drawn from tests and scales are equally useful for drawing inferences about future performance in different areas of work or in identifying the competencies required for success on a target job. At the same time, it is likely that a single measure may have implications for several aspects of job performance or the different competencies required in a job. This makes the task of integrating the assessment results and drawing inferences about a candidate's expected level of future performance quite complex. Competency in individual assessment requires careful attention and considerable skill and experience.

Drawing Inferences

While there is no clear line of demarcation between analyzing and evaluating the data on the one hand and drawing inferences on the other, it is useful to be clear about the distinction and how each is used in the assessment process. We also recognize that most of us shift back and forth from analysis and evaluation to the drawing of inferences. Nonetheless, we believe that this distinction is an important one, one that should be kept in mind throughout the process of assessment.

The following example illustrates this procedure:

Steve was a 35-year old applicant for a sales management job. His résumé indicated he had been a highly successful salesman in a related industry, a fact borne out by reference checks. In the interview he came across as a direct, hard-charging, very ambitious person who set high goals for himself and others. Psychological tests revealed him to be of above average intelligence with a strong understanding of the sales cycle and excellent closing skills. Further, the tests indicated that he was highly extroverted, strongly motivated, and very conscientious. On the other hand, both the test results and the interview data indicated that Steve was rather

tough-minded and assertive in his interactions with others. The
company prided itself on its supportive approach to employees and
its consultative style of selling, that is, helping the customer solve
problems rather than using the "hard sell," each of which were
important considerations to the company's executives. These latter
factors led to the conclusion that, while Steve would probably be a
competent sales manager in some situations, he was not a good fit
for this assignment and he was not recommended to senior management for the position.

It can readily be inferred from the available data that Steve
understands the sales process and is quite competent in applying
this understanding. Further, his approach to sales is a persuasive
one; indeed many would regard his sales style as "high pressure," a
style that is very much in keeping with his basic personality—
highly extroverted and controlling. Given that his approach to
work is an extension of who he is as a person, it is easy to infer that
he is unlikely to change that style as a sales manager. Thus we are
left with the conclusion that he is a poor fit with this particular job.

In every assessment, the candidate's prior job history is crucial to
the interpretation of assessment data. This is relevant even when the
applicant is a relatively recent addition to the workforce and thus in
the early phases of his or her career development. For instance, individuals entering the labor market as recent graduates may still be
searching for an occupational identity and, despite having made
some initial career-oriented decisions, are still quite likely to make
dramatic changes in their career paths—changes that may lead them
to leave this job. Further, despite demonstrated abilities, it is often
difficult to know how well the job under consideration will fit over
the medium term and how committed they may be to this job.

On the other hand, experienced candidates seeking positions
arrive at the assessment with considerable knowledge of the world
of work and where they fit into that world. A candidate with eight
to ten years of experience will have acquired a variety of expectations and attitudes toward the work environment that might or

might not be congruent with the present situation. While they may attempt to position themselves as relatively flexible in their willingness to meet the demands of the job, this is often not the case. Their previous work experiences may have led to the development of poor work attitudes, resistance to supervision, and other counterproductive habits.

Thus in every assessment for selection, the risks inherent in choosing a relatively unformed employee must be balanced with the risk of selecting one who is more formed but whose form will not lead to productive behavior.

Placing Values on Inferences

As we observed earlier, not all the data and the inferences based on the data are of equal importance in coming to a conclusion about the individual. The most important value should be placed on data that provides information that predicts on-the-job success. Any data point indicating that the individual has or does not have a critical competence necessary for success would receive a high value. In many cases, there also are "nice to have," but not critical, competencies. Data bearing on the presence or absence of these skills would receive lower values. And finally, there are always interesting competency data that are uncovered in the assessment process, data that usually have little or no relevance to job performance. For example, Susan is an accomplished pianist, a skill probably irrelevant to her success as a customer-service representative for a hotel chain. Some end users appreciate such information in a final report, while others prefer to have more concise reports. Both points of view are valid and should be accommodated.

The amount of available information about the individual being assessed is frequently overwhelming, even to an experienced assessor. We have found that one way of managing the unmanageable is to keep our focus on those competencies that received high ratings of importance in the job analysis. In sorting the database, it is usually very helpful to keep in mind continually the question, "Does this information bear on one of the most important competencies necessary for success on this job?" If there is not a clear-cut affirmative answer to this question, then this piece of data can be set aside.

Of equal importance in drawing inferences from the database is the organizational setting in which this job exists. As we noted in the example of Steve, the candidate for a sales management position, while he had the skills to perform the job, the manner in which he would perform the job would not fit this organization's culture. Again, the assessment process needs to place values on how the individual's work style, personality, and values fit into those of this organization. As was true of competencies, these work style issues vary in importance and need to be assessed and included in any conclusions that are drawn.

While we are not suggesting that any rigorous process for scoring the importance of these two critical areas exists—competencies and organizational fit—we do strongly believe that applying some crude metric, for example, high, medium, and low importance, to each of our inferences is an important step in the integration of the data.

While this is a deceptively simple process, it is not without its risks and pitfalls. It requires time and effort to develop the in-depth picture of the individual and an understanding of the job and its context. Not all jobs are the same, even though they share the same title, and companies are not the same, despite being in the same industry. The competent assessor must develop an understanding of each piece of this puzzle in order to put it together, a skill that is well within the capability of experienced human resources professionals.

Drawing Conclusions

The focus of the assessment process now shifts from the process of integration of assessment results to using those results to make a decision. The shift here should be toward linking these results to the purpose for conducting the assessment. It is essential that the assessor shift focus from the individual assessment data to the interpretation in a way that provides value in terms of the decisions to be made.

Interpretation begins with extracting the data evaluated as relevant, together with the inferences drawn from them and the assessment of their relative importance. This interpretative phase of the integration process is an extremely complex one and needs to be approached thoughtfully to provide the necessary understandings to the assessment process. The ultimate goal, of course, is to accurately describe the strengths and weaknesses of the candidate and to make accurate predictors about his or her performance in a particular job in a particular work setting.

Throughout this section on processing the database, we have emphasized that the goal is an accurate prediction of how well this specific individual would perform in this specific job. But this is a recommendation, not a decision. One of the perennial problems in conducting individual assessments is the frequent desire of the end users of our work—the potential employers—to have us make the decision. While our data, the inferences that we have drawn from these data, and our recommendations certainly lead to a decision, we do not regard this as a decision that we should legitimately make. Certainly the assessor is very actively involved and has a determining impact on the assessment process. At the end of the process, however, the decision should and must rest with the employer, the individual who has to live with the decision.

In selection decisions, there are few situations in which a single candidate clearly stands out as the only choice. Far more typically, at the end of the assessment of a number of individual candidates, there are several who could be considered as suitable for filling the job, each with a particular array of strengths and weaknesses. It is always the management's responsibility to weigh these options in terms of the relative assets and liabilities that each candidate brings and the needs of the organization for those strengths and its resources to compensate for the weaknesses.

The following example from our experience neatly illustrates this point with the case of filling a first-line manager-level position in a consumer-products plant:

> The first candidate had a poor understanding of the supervisory role and limited knowledge of good supervisory practices. Her score on a test of the knowledge of good supervisory practices—a specific job competence—indicated that she simply did not understand what a supervisor does or recognize how and when to monitor and manage a group of people in a goal-oriented fashion. The second candidate scored high on the knowledge of good supervisory practices test, but the personality tests and the behavioral-based interview indicated the person lacked the personal forcefulness to take charge and be firm when necessary. This second candidate probably would have difficulty in implementing what she knew about good supervisory practice in order to control and direct the work group's efforts. Finally, the third candidate also had a solid understanding of the basics of supervision, as well as having a personality that would allow her to step forward and be firm when necessary, but this person had a poorly developed sense of personal responsibility—a lack of conscientiousness. Consequently, she would have trouble completing work efforts that were goal oriented, not to mention difficulties in monitoring and managing the work of a group.

In an overall or summary evaluation, we would have three candidates for whom we reach the same conclusion, albeit for very different reasons. Of course, in different contexts, any one of these three candidates may actually be more or less attractive overall. If the first candidate has the opportunity to shadow another strong supervisor on the shop floor in order to learn and develop the competencies indicated by knowledge of good supervisory practices on the job, she could become a better possibility. If the position involves managing a very cohesive work group, with well-established roles and little history of contention, then the second candidate might be a better fit; and so forth.

In this example it is unlikely that the assessor would have the necessary information that would enable him or her to choose the most appropriate candidate, but the end user should have such information immediately available. What the end user often does not have is the problem-solving approach required to resolve this dilemma, a skill that the assessor needs to now bring to bear. The assessor's role becomes one of facilitating problem solving rather than making a simple recommendation, a far more valuable asset to the end user. Sorting out the necessary action steps in such situations requires the active collaboration of the assessor and the end user.

Once a decision is reached, the assessor and the client may need to consider several additional questions, especially when there is no neat, precise cutoff point in their relationship. For example, the candidate may be hired and the client may ask the assessor to develop and implement a training and development process for the newly hired individual. The extent of any continuing interaction will depend on the extent of the knowledge and understanding of both the assessor and the client in shifting the assessor to a different role as a consultant for training and development. We will return to this issue of the changing role of the assessor in Chapter Six.

To be successful in this additional arena, the assessor must develop an in-depth, personal knowledge of the organization and its future plans. The assessor needs to understand such issues, not as a technician, but at a deeper, more personal level as a valued, knowledgeable external resource—a position that is developed only by regular interaction with the client organization and its management and human resources personnel.

Summary

The individual assessment process involves creating a database, interpreting and integrating the information in the database, and making recommendations. In working through this process, it is always critical to keep the requirements for success on this particular job in mind in selecting the instruments, making inferences, weighting those inferences, and making the recommendations.

A number of sources of information can be included in the database for an individual assessment: a review of the résumé; interview information; results of psychological testing, including measures of personality, specific job competencies, cognitive ability, management and leadership skills, and honesty/integrity; work products; job samples; and observed behavior. Choosing among the possible measures to use is always a function of the requirements of the job under scrutiny.

These data then need to be analyzed, inferences drawn from them, and values placed on the inferences. Finally, conclusions need to be drawn. Only the client—the end user—can use the necessary information to understand and implement the tradeoffs in making a final decision—a decision that always should be made by the end user. How that information should be communicated to that end user is the focus of the next chapter.

Chapter Six

Reporting Individual Assessment Results

Reporting the results of an individual assessment to the client—the end user—is a process that requires careful planning and, on occasion, discussion and negotiation with the client. One question that often arises is the identity of the client. When conducting assessments as an internal human resources (HR) specialist, this question usually does not arise. A manager submits a request for a new hire and the internal HR specialist usually has ready access to that manager in order to raise whatever questions need to be answered. The form and content of the final report on the assessments necessary to fill that job are usually specified by organizational policy, or at least by custom. But this clarity often is not present when the assessment(s) are to be conducted by an external assessor.

Often, it is not the line manager who contacts the external assessor but rather an HR specialist who then serves as the liaison between the line manager and the consultant assessor. These HR specialists often are reluctant to allow any direct contact between the consultant and the line manager, such contact being seen as an intrusion on their turf. The filtering of the information that can occur under these circumstances leads not only to problems in defining the issues at stake but also to different expectations about the form and content of the final report. Our recommendation is that, whenever possible, try to gain direct access to the person(s) who is (are) the true end users, those who will make the final decision. At the end of the process, having such direct communication can avoid a great deal of trouble.

The Focus of a Final Report

The purpose of the assessment plays a major role in determining the focus of the final report. An assessment conducted as part of developing a training and development plan for an individual will focus on both the individual's potential for rather immediate new assignments and the person's capacity for future advancement. Since such individuals already may be well-known to the organization, many of the details that must be included in a report on an outside applicant for a position usually are not necessary.

The focus of a selection report will always be on the individual's strengths and weaknesses for filling a specified job, the requirements of which are already known. While a development report also needs to focus on strengths and weaknesses, there often is no specific job under consideration; rather, the organization is assessing its bench strength. Under such circumstances, the focus of the assessment is on determining the potential of the individual for training, promotion, and advancement in general, a far more nebulous target. We will return to this matter of assessments for training and development later in this chapter.

Content and Style

The content and form of the final report should always be a matter of negotiation between the assessor and the end user, part of the initial contracting process. This is true for both internal HR specialists and external consultants. What does the end user expect in a final report, in what form, and when? While clients generally expect longer, more detailed reports as the level of the job rises in the organizational hierarchy, this is not always the case. Some clients are quite explicit in their expectations for a short, bare-bones report, preferably in graphic form that does not require them to do much thinking. Other clients also desire such reports but are much less explicit in their expectations. Part of the assessor's task in negotiating the contract to conduct individual assessments is to determine the preferences of the client about the report and then decide whether these preferences are congruent with the assessor's preferred style. Obviously there is always room for some negotiation about such matters, but they should be addressed in the first instance, not left for the end stage of the assessment process.

Form of the Report

Ideally, communicating the results of an individual assessment process should involve a written report in a previously agreed-on structure and level of detail *and* an open discussion of the report between the assessor and the end user. But this ideal is far too rare in actual practice. More frequently the client wants only a minimal report, one that is easily digested, that does not require much thought or effort on his or her part. One of the roles that we often have had to fill is to educate the client about the potential usefulness of an individual assessment and how a collaborative relationship between the assessor and the client can ease many management problems in the human resources arena.

Obviously, some form of reporting is always required in order to communicate the results of an assessment to the user of the report and we now turn to the possible range of such reports. Reports can be as simple as a few words orally communicating the recommendation to accept or reject the candidate on the one hand to a twenty- or thirty-page narrative, including charts and graphs, followed by an extensive discussion of these data. As we noted, it is the client who determines the extent of reporting, but clients typically do not know about the range of report options; it is the assessor's responsibility to educate the client about the possibilities. We have found that actually showing a client a variety of different reports that represent different levels of content and format is a practical way of helping the client decide what is wanted in a specific assessment.

A Caveat

There is one caveat: the assessor should *not* allow the end user to choose the brief verbal report without any written documentation as the regular form for assessment reports. The absence of any written record places the organization and the assessor at risk of having no defense against a legal challenge of their hiring practices. There is no question that, without a written record to support hiring decisions, any defense against such a challenge is on very shaky grounds.

Reporting Options

In general, however, several format options for reporting the testing portion of an assessment are available, ranging from a single line graph or bar chart to a computer-generated, test-score profile, to a listing of test scores in percentiles or other normative formats. Some of these reports now are based on quite elaborate and esoteric statistical procedures. Such reports, however, can expand the computer-based profile with an accompanying narrative, and finally to the unique report, designed specifically for this assessment, that contains both extensive quantitative and narrative information.

Obviously, as we move from the brief to the lengthy, from the simple to the complex, the costs in both time and effort increase, as does the financial cost. As a result of an awareness of the costs involved, the length and complexity of assessment reports are clearly a function of the level of a specific job in the organizational hierarchy. The higher in the hierarchy, the more important and critical the job, the more the organization needs to allocate precious resources to fill that job.

Report Standardization

In the interest of enhancing the validity of assessment reports and their usefulness to the end user, we would argue that some degree of standardization in the format of assessment reports is an important requirement. While some standardization of reports is important to provide a uniform frame of reference across jobs and organizations, we are not suggesting a lock-step approach. Rather, we recommend that the standardized format presented in Exhibit 6.1 on the next page be seen as a flexible one, one that can be adapted to the realities of the particular assessment process and the long-term preferences of the assessor.

Section 1. The assessment report should include four sections, beginning with the Orienting Information. It should begin by clearly identifying the person being assessed, including a brief physical description, the position for which the person is being assessed, and a report on the individual's overall response to the assessment process, including pointing out any special circumstances that would have bearing on the interpretation of assessment information. When the person being assessed is a current employee and the purpose of the assessment is potential for promotion or development, there is no need for extensive identifying information. Finally, included in this first section is a listing of the various data sources used in the assessment, including the names of the psychological tests.

The observations made of the individual during the assessment process are an important part of this first section. How readily the individual found his or her way to the assessment, responses to the receptionist, and how the individual expressed any resistance or discomfort with or resentment of the assessment process are all potentially useful bits of information about this person. On occasion, candidates will make such statements as, "I've been through this at least seven times in the past" or "You know, I really don't believe in any of this psychological mumbo-jumbo." This information needs to be recorded in this first section of the assessment report, since it may well bear on the test results and their interpretation. These are facts or considerations that the end user needs to know early in reading the assessment report, as it colors the information that follows.

Exhibit 6.1. A Recommended Report Format

I. Orienting Information

   A. Identifying Data

      This section begins with the person's name, age, and other important identifying information, including a brief physical description.

   B. Referral Request

      In this section the reason(s) for the assessment are detailed, together with identification of the referring official.

   C. Database

      The various sources of information, including the names of the tests used, the number, length, and dates of any interviews conducted, resumes or application blanks reviewed, letter of recommendation, and any other sources of information involved should be listed.

   D. Observations

      This section includes a brief description of the individual's responses to the various steps of the assessment process. Only comments on job-related behaviors should be included.

   E. Special Circumstances

      If there are any special circumstances that might bear on the validity of the results of this assessment, such as arriving very late and thus being rushed to complete the materials, difficulty in understanding the instructions, and so on, they should be mentioned here.

II. Functional Analysis

   (*Note:* For reports on entry-level positions, in order to keep the report brief, we often combine Sections II and III.)

A. Personal/Interpersonal Functioning

The emphasis of this section is on how the individual deals with other people. Included would be a description of the individual's usual mode of dealing with others as well as an analysis of the circumstances that change that behavior, such as stress. The implications of the individual's level of social functioning for overall job performance also needs to be included in this section.

B. Intellectual Functioning

The individual's level of intellectual or cognitive ability, as well as the strategies the individual uses for problem solving, should be covered in this section. The report should also compare the individual's level of cognitive ability with that of peers. Also included should be an analysis of the person's ability to learn new material, style of thinking, and capacity for reasoning and problem solving.

C. Work Motivation

The emphasis in this section should be on the person's reasons for working, his or her level of energy, endurance, and the type of rewards that motivate him or her, as well as the sense of urgency for getting work done. Also of interest would be how well the individual is adjusted to the requirements and constraints involved in functioning successfully at work, especially in this organizational setting.

III. The Person/Job Fit

A. Personal/Interpersonal Characteristics

This competency area includes the interactions required for initiating and developing relations with superiors, peers, subordinates, and others, both within and outside the organization, as well as with customers, vendors, and members of the general public. This competency includes the ability to work effectively with others in a team.

Exhibit 6.1. A Recommended Report Format, Cont'd.

B. Problem Solving

The ability to recognize, identify, and analyze/evaluate conditions, issues, or characteristics of data and of operations are critical to this competency, as well as analyzing and resolving troubled interpersonal relationships and other situations that require management attention to preserve or enhance organization effectiveness.

C. Planning and Orchestrating

This competency area includes the analysis of business operations to identify the components, sequence, and priority for actions. This ability involves assigning or delegating authority and monitoring performance to achieve efficiency and effectiveness in immediate operations as well as consistency in order to implement long-range plans and goals.

D. Work Orientation and Adaptation

The individual's approach to work and his or her ability to recognize and accommodate the requirements for success in this job in this organization are the focus of this requirement, that is, the person and work environment fit or interaction.

E. Technical and Analytical Skills

Such competencies are required for many responsible positions in the technical/analytical industries that involve quantitative thinking and analysis. The competency involves the person's ability to understand complex quantitative problems and relationships among intangibles as a basis for developing decision strategies and rules.

F. Supervisory Skills

This competency involves knowledge of good supervisory practices and the ability to implement such knowledge successfully, as well as to adapt to changing conditions and circumstances requiring leadership actions.

G. Sales and Marketing

Such competency may be specific to jobs in sales/sales management and marketing or may be required of all managers, including supervisors. This competence includes the knowledge and ability to implement the basic sales functions, including prospecting, qualifying, handling resistance and objections, integrating information, and closing.

IV. Conclusions and Recommendations

This section should detail the most important strengths and weakness for filling this job and should clearly flow from the preceding sections of the report. The recommendations must be based on these conclusions and highlight the tradeoffs inherent in employing this individual.

The key emphasis in recording such observations is to ensure that the assessor considers a number of questions about this person and the observed behavior, such questions as, "What kind of person is this?" "What kind of person will say such things about him- or herself?" "What kind of impression is this person trying to achieve?" Such information can go a long way in helping to develop an understanding of the person's approach to situations and his or her underlying values. Remember, the goal of the individual assessment practice is to obtain an understanding of the individual's strengths and weaknesses, and all data is grist for the mill.

Section 2. The second section consists of a functional analysis that describes the applicant in general terms along three dimensions with a minimum of evaluative comment: (a) Personal/Interpersonal Functioning; (b) Intellectual Functioning; and (c) Work Motivation. Thus, the focus of this section is descriptive rather than evaluative. These descriptions provide the basis for the competency evaluations that comprise the next section. It is important to note that this section covers the person's performance in the three thematic areas, not in a test-by-test fashion.

It is imperative that the separate bits of information in each area of functioning be aggregated and studied separately to avoid the information from one area contaminating that from another. Aggregating and organizing the data in each of these three components completes the task of this section, preparation for interpreting the descriptive results.

Section 3. In the third section of the report, the individual's perceived competence in each critical area is compared to the necessary level of competency previously identified as required for job success—the Person/Job Fit. For each competency required for job success, a short (forty-to-fifty word) evaluative statement is appropriate. The statement should summarize the relevant data on which the inference of competence is drawn, that is, what data support the inferred level of this competence. This section of the report should include the assessor's rating of the individual on each of the critical competencies for success on this job using the five-point scale presented in Appendix C.

The example of competencies presented in the third section of the recommended format is summarized for a first-line-manager level position (Appendix D); it represents an aggregate of the competencies typically required in such positions. It is offered as a sample of a common set of competencies that guide individual assessments. Obviously, jobs at different levels in the organizational hierarchy would have different competencies. For example, production-type jobs would have fewer and less complex competencies, while higher-level management and executive-level jobs would have more and higher-level competencies. The three sample reports in Appendices F, G, and H do provide examples of competencies at three different levels in organizational hierarchies.

Section 4. The fourth and final section of the report contains the assessor's conclusions and recommendations, highlighting the person's strengths and weaknesses as well as an overall, global rating of the applicant's suitability for this position. In drawing these conclusions and making a recommendation, it is important to be clear that they flow directly from the competence ratings previously shown in Exhibit 4.1.

Sample assessment reports utilizing this model are presented in Appendices F, G, and H at the end of this volume. Appendix F is a report on an entry-level position; Appendix G, a first-line management/supervisory job; and Appendix H, an executive position. It is important to note that these reports use the above model but that each report is targeted to a specific end user and thus deviates to some degree from that model.

Drafting a Final Report

To facilitate writing a final report, the assessor should review the entire data set and all of the experiences in dealing with this person, then consider how these data bear on the issue of what the client needs to know about this individual and his or her level of functioning. Writing a narrative report that integrates all of the relevant assessment data that can be used to answer the client's questions is a time-consuming and demanding process. Fortunately, it is one that becomes easier with practice.

Keeping in mind the interactions among the database, which is the foundation for the assessment report, the description of the individual in the three areas of functioning, and the competency analysis is essential. In drafting a final report, it is usually necessary to go back and forth between these elements as the writing progresses. Integrating the job requirements with the competency analysis requires considerable skill, skill that takes time to develop. Assessors first need to expand their understanding of the assessment data. As this understanding develops, the focus can shift to improving the understanding of the individual in terms of the data and then in terms of job/person competency fit.

Since assessment reports are written for different jobs at many different levels, it is necessary to carefully select and use the appropriate normative reference or comparison group data in reporting the test results. For some tests, only a single normative group is available, and the interpretation thus is the same for all individuals. The results from such single-norm tests should be interpreted with extreme caution, as they often can fail to identify large differences among various demographic and occupational groups that should be taken into consideration in interpreting these results.

Other tests have multiple sets of normative data, and the report always should be based on the most relevant group. For example, measures of mechanical aptitude typically will have a variety of available norms with substantial and significant differences in the score distributions for different groups. College-educated mechanical engineers will score much higher than assembly-line workers, even though this ability is an important predictor of success for both groups. Only by using the appropriate norm or comparison group can we make a valid prediction, and that norm group should be specified in the final report. This can only be accomplished if the assessor develops and maintains an in-depth knowledge of each instrument used by careful study of the latest manuals for the tests employed.

Drawing Conclusions and Making Recommendations

The first three sections of an assessment report typically are rich with data. The conclusions section provides the assessor with an opportunity to highlight the most pertinent data that bear on this person's suitability to fill the job. These conclusions should be presented in the order of importance, with the most important information presented first. It is important to keep this portion of the report brief and not to simply repeat the data previously provided.

Whether an assessor should just report, describe, and recommend or should assume an active decision-making role is the subject of some controversy. As we noted previously, we strongly support the former role, as only the end user must live with the consequences of the final decision. Realistically, however, it is common for an assessor to have the power to reject an applicant, but not to override a positive decision. In most situations, the client wants a clear description of the individual and his or her strengths and weaknesses and some discussion of what must be done if the individual were to be hired to build on strengths and compensate for any deficiencies.

The individual assessment process does not occur in a vacuum. Assessments often are requested in a high-pressure environment. For example, there is an immediate need to fill an important vacancy or concern about what to do with an incumbent who clearly has become derailed. How you craft your final report—how you describe the individual and analyze the person/job fit—will have considerable impact on what happens to that person. The assessor needs to be quite careful to maintain equanimity, to be a constant, steadying influence, one who will not be influenced by the present situation into making hurried, rash judgments.

A Decision-Making Model

These are several approaches for making a personnel recommendation. One such approach is the multiple-hurdles strategy approach, which is a *non-compensatory model*. In this model a strength does not compensate for a weakness and the individual must clear each hurdle by demonstrating an adequate level of each competence. On the other hand, the *compensatory approach* evaluates a candidate on each competence, the competency ratings are averaged, and a recommendation or a decision is made on the basis of the average rating. Thus, strength in one competence can compensate for a weakness in another. Depending on which decision-making approach is used, different candidates conceivably could be recommended for the job.

Each of these approaches has its own assets and limitations. In the non-compensatory model, candidate-processing costs are somewhat lower because the number of candidates at each subsequent stage will be reduced. Also, remedial and training costs for new hires will be contained. On the other hand, recruiting costs will be higher, as will be the potential waste of talent. When there is an ample supply of candidates in the market, however, this will not be of particular concern.

In the compensatory model, costs for processing each candidate will be higher, but fewer applicants will be needed. The deficiencies or weaknesses of a specific candidate may require some remedial effort, but, if those deficiencies are indeed remediable, they can be addressed during the early period of employment. The compensatory model also has an obvious advantage in a tight labor market when relatively few applicants are available.

Under some circumstances, a *composite model* is the most appropriate approach to decision making—one involving both the compensatory and non-compensatory approaches. In the composite model, the non-compensatory approach is used to set minimum qualifications that are used to screen out unqualified applicants. For those who possess the minimum qualifications, additional assessment data is collected in order to evaluate their relative strengths and weaknesses, using the compensatory approach. Given an adequate supply of candidates in the labor market, the composite approach is much preferred over the other two.

When, however, this is not the case, there are at least two different ways of deciding whether to use the compensatory or non-compensatory approach. One is to attempt to clarify these choices when the scope of the assessment process is being negotiated between the client and the assessor. The other way of resolving this issue is for the assessor to write a final report covering the several candidates and spell out the recommendations stemming from each of these two approaches. This allows the end user to decide both on the decision-making rule and on the final outcome; thus the choice will better reflect the organization's preferences and better match the prevailing local conditions.

It should be noted, however, that there are some weaknesses or limitations for which there probably is no compensatory mechanism. We should include among those a history of serious legal problems, such as bad debts, fraud, and repeated bankruptcies, untreated problems of alcoholism, complaints of sexual harassment, and other serious behavioral problems. When such issues are identified in the course of an individual assessment, they should raise serious questions about the suitability of this candidate for the job.

A Forty-Question Checklist

Our approach for reporting assessment results described in this chapter has evolved over several years. In preparing reports for the end-user client we have found that it is important to make certain that this final report is comprehensive and addresses all the important issues involved in the assessment. Implicit in these issues are critical questions that need to be answered in the report, questions that the client expects to be answered. Exhibit 6.2 provides a final report checklist in the form of forty questions.

Obviously, very few instances exist in which a report would need to address each and every one of the questions. But we have found that using such a checklist as the basis for deciding whether we have done what we have been contracted to do is a valuable quality-control mechanism. In other words, after we believe that we have completed our report, we review this checklist to remind ourselves of issues that may have been addressed only partially or not at all.

Reviewing these questions and answering the pertinent ones in any given assessment report will help ensure a degree of quality in that final report and increase end-user satisfaction both with the report and the entire assessment process.

Computer-Generated Reports

The assessment process described in this and the preceding chapters involves combining information about an individual with information about jobs and job requirements in a narrative report. However, it is possible to take a rather different approach to reporting of assessment results—the automated or standardized computer-generated report. This widely used approach simply interprets data using statistical algorithms that mechanically produce such reports.

Exhibit 6.2. Final Report Checklist

Orienting Information

1. What is the individual's full name?

2. Who authorized the assessment?

3. What was the purpose for the assessment?

4. What documents the specifications for this assessment?

5. What occurred during the assessment process that the end user needs to know about?

6. Was feedback about the assessment provided to the person being assessed?

7. Does the structure of the report implicitly address the purpose of the assessment?

Personal/Interpersonal Functioning

8. Does the report adequately describe this person?

9. How does this individual usually interact with others?

10. What factors or conditions influence this person's job-related personal/interpersonal behaviors?

11. What are the implications of this person's personal/interpersonal style on his or her job performance?

12. What factors might influence his or her personal/interpersonal behavior in this work setting?

13. What factors influence this individual's personal/interpersonal behavior involving fellow employees and others?

14. What are the factors that affect this person's organizational behavior?

15. Does this person's personal/interpersonal behavior impact his or her intellectual functioning?

16. Does personal/interpersonal functioning have implications for his or her work motivation and aspirations?

17. Are there any overriding personal/interpersonal considerations that have implications for job or organizational behavior?

18. Is this person's personal/interpersonal functioning helpful for training and development?

Intellectual Functioning

19. What is the individual's general level of cognitive functioning?

20. What is this person's thinking style? Is this person an analytical or an intuitive thinker?

21. How broad is this individual's general knowledge base?

22. Are there any major limitations in intellectual functioning?

23. What is this individual's approach to work in terms of problem identification and problem solving?

24. What is this individual's general approach to work, in terms of such factors as detail orientation, level of endurance and persistence, and intellectual curiosity?

25. What is the individual's job-relevant skill base?

26. To what extent has the individual benefited from prior work experiences?

27. Does this individual have a well-defined approach to job performance?

28. Are there special considerations that are related to this individual's intellectual functioning for this specific job?

29. Are there any specific gaps in this person's cognitive functioning that are likely to affect his or her job performance?

Work Motivation

30. What are the individual's primary motives that influence his or her current job performance?

31. What motivations are likely to influence the person's future job performance?

Exhibit 6.2. Final Report Checklist, Cont'd.

32. What are this individual's level of energy, endurance, and sense of urgency?

33. What are the individual's aspirations: how far would he or she like to advance?

34. How will the individual respond to training or on-the-job mentoring or coaching?

35. What is this individual's level of personal adjustment, sense of self-sufficiency, sense of competence?

36. Do the individual's motivations or aspirations constitute factors in either personal/interpersonal or cognitive functioning?

37. Does this person have long-term aspirations?

38. Is this a mature individual?

39. What level of self-awareness or personal insight does this individual have?

40. How readily does this individual adapt to new work and organizational demands?

The most sophisticated of these computerized systems do require line managers and human resources specialists to identify the job to be filled. The computer uses this information to select and administer the appropriate assessment instruments to the candidates based on previously stored generic models of that job. Typically, the computer program generates a visual report on the degree to which each candidate has each of the necessary competencies, a listing of the candidates in rank order of suitability for the job, and a listing of interview questions for follow-up by the client's staff. These computer outputs typically are based on using the insights of a single individual or a small team with extensive expertise using a particular test measure. While this process produces an automated report, the content of which is evaluative in nature and similar or comparable in content to that produced by many practitioners, there are no professional observations and none of the insights that can flow from such observations being included.

As we have noted previously, the major problem with this approach is that, all too often, such reports are based on suitability for filling a class of jobs rather than a specific job in a specific workplace. Nor can the computer program integrate the findings from a variety of tests, especially if they are from different testing publishers. In other words, these computer-based interpretative programs do not take into consideration the issues inherent in working on a particular job. While such reports clearly do have their place in employment screening, they lack the targeted specificity and customization with which this book has been concerned.

Individual Assessment for Development

Up to this point we have concentrated on conducting individual assessments for selection—both for initial job selection and for promotion. This focus reflects the fact that the overwhelming majority of assessments are conducted for such selections. But there is an emerging interest in using individual assessments for other purposes, often as an early step in training and development or in team building or outplacement as well.

Assessment for Development

Most often, the focus of an assessment report in the context of development needs is on planning for the future rather than on the selection decision of the present. This shift to both a broader context and a more distant point of view clearly suggests that assessment for selection may simply be the first stage in the process of continuous employee development. In effect, the employment decision represents a transition point at which the focus shifts from the assessment report together with the selection decision based on that report to the implications of the report for the longer-term future of that employee.

In addition to this expanded area of focus, assessment for the purpose of development has two other differences from those for selection. When conducting assessments for selection, we are comparing the individual with a known set of job competencies; that is, the question is how well this individual fits the competency specifications that have been set for filling this specific job. While immediate training needs may be specified in the selection report, the focus remains on the hiring decision.

Assessing an individual in terms of his or her long-term potential usually is cast in terms of general potential for future advancement—identifying younger, less experienced individuals as "fast-trackers" to be groomed for senior ranks, for example—rather than on what training and development might be necessary to increase that individual's potential for successfully filling a specific future job. This is quite a different task, as we do not have a specific template against which to compare the individual, but rather are asked for an evaluation for a yet-to-be-identified more senior position and at some nonspecified time in the future.

A comprehensive implementation of this strategy would begin by conducting both a future-oriented job analysis (how today's senior jobs may change over time) and the relevant competency analysis for those revised jobs. This formidable task would then be followed by an effort to predict who among current employees might develop those competencies. We will return to this issue of future-oriented job analysis at the end of the chapter. Meanwhile, this lack of specificity about a future job suggests the need for caution in drawing firm conclusions in any such report. Furthermore, strong performers at one level are not always able to meet the challenges of more responsible positions successfully. While we support efforts to identify and give special opportunities to those who appear to be especially talented, we must also be careful not to urge advancement beyond a person's capacity, particularly when that future job is relatively unknown.

Who receives the completed report is an additional important difference between selection and developmental assessments. Selection reports are prepared for the specific client—the person with hiring authority and perhaps one or two others with related responsibility. The person being assessed, the subject of the report, is *not* among those individuals. When the purpose is developmental, however, the person who was assessed, the subject of the report, is the most important recipient, perhaps also including such others as that person's supervisor and appropriate HR staff.

Providing the subject with his or her assessment report raises some important considerations about both its content and style. While selection reports typically regard weaknesses as disqualifiers, the development report must approach each such weakness or limitation as a developmental opportunity. Thus, in pointing out each such weakness the report necessarily should suggest some fairly specific action steps that would address this weakness, such as mentoring, formal training, professional counseling, and so on. There is also a tendency for some developmental assessment reports to gloss over the negative impact of such limitations for the individual's future in order to "spare his feelings." A report that "pulls its punches" in such a fashion does not do justice to the subject. Rather, writing a well-balanced report, highlighting equally both the individual's strengths and limitations, is the fairest and most professional approach.

An individual assessment for development purposes must involve painting a broad picture of the individual, highlighting the person's strengths and weakness in broad, general terms. But strengths and weaknesses do not exist in a vacuum; rather, they need to be considered in the context of a particular organization, and every organization prizes some strengths more than others, while having less tolerance for some weaknesses than others. Thus, organizational culture provides a framework for conducting individual assessments for development, directing the focus to an identification of those strengths that the individual most needs to enhance and those weaknesses that most seriously need to be remedied.

In one such example from our practice, the organization's culture highly prized a combative approach to decision making—one was expected to fiercely advocate one's position in staff meetings—and a willingness to compromise too quickly was always regarded as a sign of personal weakness. Our client, a middle-level manager, found this requirement very difficult to meet. Mild-mannered and introverted, argumentation was not in his skill set and, as a consequence, the unit he managed did not receive the resources it needed and he was undervalued by his superiors. His development assessment focused on clarifying the reasons for this reticence and identifying a variety of resources to help him overcome this reluctance, including increasing his negotiating skills, improving the volume and quality of his speech, and providing regular mentoring sessions that provided him both with skills and support to improve his performance.

Mentoring

Mentoring is a formal relationship between an individual with significant experience (mentor) and another (mentee) in which each develops professionally through the transfer of experience and the opportunity to seek alternative perspectives. Mentoring or coaching programs have become an important part of the training and development program of many organizations. The mentor can be a more senior manager or executive, a human resources specialist, or an external consultant. Substantial research (for example, Chao, 1997; Chao, Walz, & Gardner, 1992; Kram, 1985) has shown that mentoring is an effective enhancer of performance and positively impacts the salary level, promotion rate, and job satisfaction of mentees, as well as other measures of job success.

Regardless of the background and orientation of the mentor, the mentoring process can be greatly enhanced when it is based on an individual assessment that provides a guide to the mentor about the developmental needs of the individual. Such an assessment should include information about any gaps in knowledge and skills that require addition formal education or training, any cross-functional assignments necessary to broaden the individual's experiential base, and, perhaps most importantly, personal/interpersonal characteristics that might inhibit or block this individual's career advancement. This is one of the instances in which one or more of the measures of leadership listed in Appendix I is often useful as part of the assessment process.

One psychological inventory that we have found especially useful in this regard is the Hogan Development Survey (Hogan & Hogan, 1997), especially when the person being assessed is encountering some on-the-job problems. Based on the research at the Center for Creative Leadership on why executives fail—get *derailed* in the Center's terminology—and based on the test results from over two thousand employees, managers, and executives, the Hogan Development Survey (HDS) provides scores on eleven scales, each of which describes a non-functional behavioral pattern leading to on-the-job problems, even derailment.

The HDS report serves as the linchpin of the developmental process and serves as the focus of the initiation of the mentoring process. An inspection of the HDS manual reveals that these eleven scales are not completely independent, but they do highlight behaviors that need the individual's attention if success is to be attained. The HDS manual also identifies the specific psychiatric personality disorders that may be involved at the most extreme levels of these behaviors.

The eleven scale names, however, are euphemisms for these counter-productive behaviors in order to increase the likelihood that the individual will not reject his or her HDS report out-of-hand when it is received. The eleven HDS scales together with a parenthetical and more hard-hitting description of the underlying behavioral issues involved follows: (1) excitable (volatile; moody); (2) skeptical (distrustful; negative; suspicious); (3) cautious (overly careful; wary; guarded); (4) reserved (detached; aloof; uncommunicative); (5) leisurely (passive-aggressive; overly independent;

non-responsive); (6) bold (arrogant; grandiose; overly self-confident); (7) mischievous (risk taker; playful; anti-social); (8) colorful (melo-dramatic; animated; histrionic); (9) imaginative (eccentric; odd; peculiar): (10) diligent (perfectionist; meticulous; inflexible); and (11) dutiful (dependent; compliant; submissive). In each case, the higher the scale score, the greater the tendency, with percentile scores above 90 suggesting that this behavior places the person at high risk.

The following case illustrates the potential usefulness of the HDS in mentoring:

> Carl was a 48-year old, highly successful bench scientist at a large pharmaceutical corporation. With a Ph.D. degree from an Ivy-league university and a dozen years of experience at the company, he had been promoted to be market manager for one of the drugs that he had help developed. He was referred to an external consul-tant, as he was having extreme difficulty in meeting his new respon-sibilities. To initiate the mentoring process, Carl completed the HDS as part of a more comprehensive test battery.
>
> On the HDS, Carl scored in the High Risk category on the Caution and Diligent scales and in the Moderate Risk category on the Leisurely and Reserved scales. His scores clearly indicated that his behavioral style had enabled him to be successful as a scientist, where being meticulous and careful (and also somewhat aloof and remote) and basing one's decisions on strong evidence did not inhibit his success. This style, however, was antithetical to the mar-keting function. In marketing the data are naturally "squishy" (Carl's word), decisions always must be based on incomplete data, and open communications are imperative—all far outside Carl's preferred style of operating. Thus the mentoring process focused on whether Carl was willing and able to make the changes in behav-ioral style that he now understood would be necessary to succeed in his new role.
>
> Without recounting in any detail the hours spent in weighing the pros and cons of this decision, at the end of the process Carl

decided that he would be more fulfilled both personally and professionally by a return to a more scientifically oriented job. The company, eager to retain his talents, created a new position for him that was a lateral move from his marketing job and where he continues to enjoy considerable success.

The issues of job fit occur at every level of the job hierarchy and require constant attention, with individual assessments providing useful insights into the person/job fit.

Out-Placement

In these days of organizational downsizing, corporate mergers and acquisitions, and generalized organizational turbulence, many individuals are being released by their employers, some through no fault of their own. As part of the separation process, many of these people, especially those at the managerial and executive levels, are offered out-placement counseling. Such counseling is another venue where individual assessments can provide invaluable information to the process.

The first issue that needs to be addressed in out-placement counseling is whether the separation was based on poor performance, egregious behavior, or simply bad luck. One of our out-placement clients was released from his position as general counsel of a large media corporation when it was acquired by an even larger company. While some of the senior executives from the acquired firm were retained, our client was not that lucky. The general counsel of the acquirer had a long-term, close personal relationship with his CEO, and there was no way that he would be passed over.

The counseling focus in this case was on dealing with the client's depression and sense of outrage, which were clearly apparent in his personality test results. These feelings preoccupied him and severely interfered with his willingness to begin a job search. The information provided by the individual assessment was vitally important in allowing catharsis over time and reenergizing of the client.

This case is in sharp contrast to instances in which the out-placement client has been released because of either performance or behavioral problems. Here again, an individual assessment will go a long way in illuminating the degree to which personality aberrations have played a role in getting the individual fired. When this is the case, the focus of out-placement counseling will be on confronting the person with the impact of the prior behavioral pattern on his or her career and raising the difficult question of whether or not the person has the willingness and the ability to modify these pre-existing patterns. The case of Carl cited above is but one such example, even though he was not involved in out-placement.

The role of individual assessments arguably is more important in out-placement than in any other application. The central issue in out-placement counseling is to find a person/job fit, although there is no job analysis available to judge that fit. A comprehensive assessment report should provide the counselor with a clear understanding of the client's various strengths, limitations, motivations, and so on, which should guide the counselor in discussions of the pros and cons of the various job opportunities that the client will consider. Without such an assessment, the counselor can be of little help in assisting the client in moving his or her career forward.

Team Building

Still another application of individual assessment is in team building, although in this case the assessment process is quite different from what we have been discussing. Team building is a process in which a team embarks on a process of self-assessment in order to evaluate the effectiveness of the team and thereby improve its performance. As part of this self-assessment, each team member completes some kind of a psychologically based personality measure, which is scored and then returned so that it can be used as a data point in a series of facilitated team meetings.

The facilitator usually provides the team with a lecture on the theory underlying the test and the meaning of various scores, which together serve as the formal assessment. Many of the personality tests used in team building include extensive written material that helps the team members to understand their own scores. The facilitator also may have one-on-one interpretative sessions to further each team member's understanding of his or her own scores, but the essence of this type of team-building process is for each team member to share his or her scores with the total team in order for the team to develop a better understanding of each team member's personality and how that personality impacts team effectiveness. Teams literally spend hours reviewing their successes and failures in terms of how the incompatibility of various individual personality types affected team performance. The assessment process in such team building thus is a group enterprise rather than an individual one—a major difference in methodology. The unresolved issue, however, is the degree to which such team building actually improves team performance long-term.

Most people in the workforce do not have a sophisticated conceptual or language system to describe workplace behavior and the problems that this behavior engenders. Rather, we hear lavish praise ("She's the best manager in the company") or denigration ("He's a total jerk"). There is no *Gray's Anatomy* of personality available to guide general usage. Sharing scores on personality tests in team building is one way to remedy this situation, as it provides a relatively simple theory of human behavior and a user-friendly set of constructs to use, together with a new language. The Myers-Briggs Type Indicator (MBTI) is certainly the most widely used instrument in this type of team building, despite its clear psychometric limitations (Lanyon & Goodstein, 1997).

We strongly urge the human resources mangers who typically initiate such team-building processes to make their decisions on the basis of the critical psychometric principles discussed in Chapter Three—principles that lead to predictive validity—rather than responding to the slick brochures and marketing efforts of commercial test publishers. One of our objectives in writing this book was to increase the sophistication of the field of human resources management about assessment methodology. Improving the quality of personality tests used in team building would be an excellent place to start.

Future-Oriented Job Analysis

We conclude this narrative where we began, with a discussion of the role of job analysis in individual assessment. This final issue for us to address is the shelf life of job analysis data and its application in HR activities. We typically focus attention on what is current and rarely are concerned with the past. We are, however, very much concerned with the future and the implications of the future on the process of job analyses.

While we are always concerned with both the accuracy of our selection decisions and how individuals change and develop over time, we tend to assume that a job is a job is a job—a relatively static state of affairs. Jobs do change, however, and those changes occur because of technology developments, market changes, business reorganization, including mergers, acquisitions, and downsizing, and so on. Identifying and preparing for such changes is the basis of future-oriented job analysis.

What is often unnoticed as a consequence of these changes is the unobtrusive impact of many of the collateral organizational changes that are occurring in the workplace, changes that we initially do not take into account. This is especially true of many technological changes, which can wreak havoc in ongoing operations. For example, one of our clients in a garment manufacturing operation introduced a great deal of new manufacturing equipment. As was expected, the initial impact was a dramatic decrease in productivity and an increase in defective products.

Within a year productivity and quality had clearly improved overall. But about 20 percent of the plant workforce was still unable to adjust to these changes. The cause of the problem was quickly diagnosed as a lack of literacy, that is, these employees could not read the dials on the equipment. The new equipment had dramatically changed the nature of the work, but there was no accompanying understanding of its impact on the workforce. In this example, a future-oriented job analysis should have identified these collateral changes and helped management prepare to address them.

In a similar situation in a different organization, management developed a unique and potentially more cost-effective manufacturing process using state-of-the-art technology. This manufacturing process was expected to provide the company with a very significant competitive advantage. This company was eager to proceed and to prepare for any collateral change caused by the new processes so arranged for a future-oriented job analysis to be conducted. A team of subject-matter experts conducted an intensive job analysis including both work activity and KSA components, which facilitated the design of the new jobs. This design allowed the company both to make certain that the new process was user-friendly and to train its workforce well in advance, avoiding the kind of collateral damage experienced in the first example.

The topic of future-oriented job analysis has received little attention in past years, but the pace of technological as well as societal changes makes such attention imperative. As these changes become yet more challenging, they will require increasingly more sophisticated innovations in job analysis methodology. While it is clearly impossible to predict all the changes and their impact on the workplace, many of them are discernable and can be integrated in HR planning in order to avoid future shock. Clearly, in conducting a job analysis, those involved have to keep one eye on the future and take that future into account in the identification of the critical competencies that will be necessary, both now and in the future, to whatever extent that is possible.

Summary

To repeat the underlying theme of our approach to individual assessment, the central question of any individual assessment is how well the person meets the requirements of the job. Obviously, answering this question requires a structured and standardized job analysis that identifies the essential job content in terms of work activities and the most essential competencies required for effective performance on this job. While there certainly are variations in acceptable format and writing style, the communication with the client about this person/job fit is absolutely critical and is the single most important factor in determining the usefulness of any assessment report.

Using the recommended report format helps ensure that the final report addresses the critical issues involved in most assessments. This format suggests four sections: introduction, functional analysis, person/job fit, and conclusions and recommendations. This last section should focus on the relative strengths and weaknesses of the individual, leaving the final decision to the end user. There are three decision-making models: compensatory, non-compensatory, and composite, with the last being the most preferred. Over the years we have developed a forty-item checklist that provides an additional approach to quality control of the final report.

Using individual assessments to facilitate the training and development of a person is an important next step in an ongoing assessment process. Individual assessments have been shown to be helpful in developing training and development plans for individuals, for mentoring, for out-placement, and for team building. Finally, we address the need to consider how jobs are changing, that is, how to move to a future-oriented job analysis process—a reprise of the beginning of this volume.

Over the last six chapters we have laid out a process for conducting individual assessments. The underlying rationale for this process is based on our many years of experience in conducting assessments as well as our understanding of basic psychometric principles and the empirical findings reported in the research literature. It is our earnest hope that the readers of this book, as a result of what they have read here, will be able to improve their own assessment practices, become more sophisticated purchasers of assessments, or have a better understanding of how the process of individual assessment may impact their lives.

Appendix A

Recommended Readings

The following are texts that provide a basic introduction to staffing and selection:

Fisher, C.D., Schoenfeldt, L.F., & Shaw, J.B. (1996). *Human resource management* (3rd ed.). New York: Houghton Mifflin.

Gatewood, R.D., & Field, H.S. (1998). *Human resource selection* (4th ed.). Fort Worth, TX: Dryden Press.

Heneman, H.G., III, Heneman, R.L., & Judge, T.A. (1997). *Staffing organizations* (2nd ed.). Middleton, WI: Irwin.

The following are texts that provide a basic introduction to the science of psychological testing and measurement:

Aiken, L.R. (2002). *Psychological testing and assessment* (11th ed.). New York: Pearson Allyn & Bacon.

Anastasi, A., & Urbina, S. (1996). *Psychological testing* (7th ed.). New York: Pearson Educational.

Cronbach, L.J. (1970). *Essential of psychological testing* (3rd ed.). New York: Harper and Row.

Lanyon, R.I., & Goodstein, L.D. (1997). *Personality assessment* (3rd ed.). Hoboken, NJ: John Wiley & Sons.

Prien, E.P., Schippman, J.S., & Prien, K.O. (2003). *Individual assessment as practiced in industry and consulting*. Mahwah, NJ: Lawrence Erlbaum.

Sample Position Description

Executive Secretary

Summary

The Executive Secretary works under the general supervision of the Executive Vice President. The individual in this position enters data and processes written material; files and retrieves materials; performs administrative secretarial duties; performs reception activities; receives, ships, and distributes mail and supplies; analyzes, interprets, and reports business data; performs other duties as assigned.

Duties

1. *Types and processes written material:* enters data from copy, longhand notes, or dictation; composes routine correspondence or memoranda following standard operating procedures; composes letters, memos, or other documents for the Executive Vice President's signature; prepares tables, charts, graphs, or diagrams based on data provided by other sources.

2. *Files and retrieves materials:* reviews, updates, or analyzes current status of subject; places forms, records, correspondence in the file; classifies or sorts correspondence, records, or other items

following standard office procedure; searches indices, manuals, files, or records for desired information on specific subjects; locates and retrieves files.

3. *Performs administrative duties:* notifies or reminds the Executive Vice President or other department heads of meetings, scheduled dates, specific duties, or occurrences; maintains appointment schedule for the Executive Vice President; coordinates the scheduling of meetings, facilities, or events with other individuals; investigates the source of discrepancies in documentation; prepares travel authorization and/or meeting arrangements for departmental personnel.

4. *Performs reception activities:* answers telephone and screens calls for the Executive Vice President; greets visitors to the Executive Vice President's office; answers questions or provides information directly or by telephone.

5. *Receives, ships, and distributes mail and supplies:* certifies, registers, insures, or completes forms associated with special mail services such as overnight courier or registered mail; prepares confidential documents for shipment via courier, distributes mail bulletins, memos, and reports to other employees.

6. *Analyzes, interprets, and reports business data:* prepares reports, based on information at hand, following standard departmental procedures; prepares analysis or summaries of programs, reports, specific operational items, or other data.

7. *Performs other duties as assigned.*

Competency Requirements

1. *Communication Skills:* Ability to organize and convey information orally and in documents.

2. *Work and Organization Skills:* Ability to follow through on assignments, adjust schedules, and set priorities.

3. *Scheduling and Coordinating Skills*: Skill in making arrangements, scheduling, coordinating, and orchestrating activities.

4. *Processing Written Materials*: Skill in data entry and proofing copy; knowledge of proper formats for various documents.

5. *Clerical Research and Evaluation Skills*: Knowledge of procedures to locate and obtain materials and to trace sources of errors.

6. *Work and Organization Adaptation*: Ability to pace work activities and to identify, accommodate, and adapt to the conditions or circumstances of the work and the organization and other people.

Minimum Qualifications

Completion of a two-year course of study in Secretarial Sciences at an accredited institution. A minimum of three years of full-time experience regularly involving at least four of the duty areas in the job description.

Appendix C

Introduction to Job Analysis

A job analysis is a study of the job requirements and involves following a prescribed series of steps or operations that produce a set of specifications of the competencies necessary for success on a particular job in a particular work setting.

While there are some alternative approaches to conducting a job analysis, the typical process follows a sequence of five steps. The first four involve collecting information on:

1. Work activity (WA);
2. Knowledge, skills, and ability (KSA);
3. Job performance; and
4. Work-setting characteristics.

The final step is assembling the collected data in a formal job analysis and applying it to the assessment process.

WA and KSA information usually can be collected simultaneously. Job performance data usually needs to be collected separately, as the source of these data and the techniques used to collect them are different. The job performance data are of particular importance because these data are a critical component in establishing the validity of the job analysis. While work-setting information can be gathered simultaneously with WA and KSA data, it is typically gathered independently because it comes from different sources.

From a practical standpoint, sufficient data often already exist to describe adequately the necessary WAs and KSAs required for many jobs. Such data can be obtained from narrative job descriptions as well as from previously published studies of job performance. For example, both WA and KSA data for clerical or administrative and general management jobs are readily available in the published literature. Nonetheless, some interviews and/or observation are helpful for confirming the suitability of and refining such generic descriptions.

Collecting the Work Activity (WA) Data

The objective of this initial process is to identify and define the WAs involved in a specific job. Conducting a series of unstructured interviews with people familiar with the job, followed by direct observation, is a good way to begin collecting this job information. Obviously higher-level jobs will have a greater range and number of WAs. Focus-group interviews about a specific job provide the information needed to identify and establish sequentially both the WAs and KSAs that are critical to this job.

The discussion should be initiated with a description of its purpose, highlighting how this job analysis will be used. Participants should be prompted initially to define the job functions and their scope in terms of WAs, that is, to specify exactly what the person needs to do on a regular basis in performing this job. A flip chart or a large blackboard is useful for recording the data, with the group leader continuing to probe until the WAs are adequately described. Any editing of the WA statements should be done later; the intent at this time is to generate content while the group has this job clearly in focus. Once the WAs for the job are established, the *importance* of each of these needs to be rated.

First, consider whether a WA is or is not part of the job. If it is not part of the job, rate "0." Second, if the WA is part of the job, decide how important it is for fully effective performance. Use the following scale to make your judgments:

0   This WA is never done and is not part of this job.

1   This WA is of only minor importance relative to other job activities.

2   This WA is fairly important relative to other job activities.

3   This rating indicates that the WA is important and is an essential function for fully effective job performance.

4   This WA is very important for fully effective job performance.

5   This rating indicates that the WA is one of the most important and essential functions for fully effective job performance.

Identifying and Collecting Knowledge, Skills, and Abilities (KSA) Data

Once the WAs are specified, the KSAs necessary for performing each of the WAs needs to be identified. For example, for a first-line manager job, "Originate and conduct staff meetings to exchange information, establish priorities, develop solutions for emerging problems" is a highly important WA. To perform this WA successfully, a supervisor needs to possess a number of different KSAs, including verbal communication skills, teamwork skills, analytic ability, project-planning ability, business knowledge, and general supervisory skills. Each of these KSAs would be broken down further into more specific elements. For example, supervisory skills would include recognizing the situational restrictions on his or her role, willingness to act on information, skills in delegation and follow-up, and so on.

Incumbents, subject-matter experts, and/or professional job analysts can make identification of the associated KSAs. Since these KSAs are the basis for the specification of the necessary competencies to fill this job, it is *absolutely essential* that the identification and definition of KSAs be done correctly, regardless of who does them. Moreover, it is important to understand how each of these terms is defined.

Knowledge is the foundation upon which abilities and skills are built and is defined as an organized body of information, usually of a factual or procedural nature, which, if applied, makes adequate performance of the job possible. For example, understanding how an internal combustion engine works is an important knowledge in successfully doing auto repairs. It should be noted, however, that possession of a bit of knowledge does not ensure its proper application.

Skill is defined as proficiency in the manual, verbal, or mental manipulation of people, ideas, or things. A skill must be demonstrable, and possession of a skill implies a level of proficiency or a standard that must be met. For example, reading gauges and dials is a critical skill in doing auto repairs.

Ability is defined as the present capacity to perform a job function, to execute an activity by relying on the underlying knowledge base and adequate application of skills. Abilities differ from skills in that the ability to perform a job function, for example, tuning up the engine of a car, involves a number of different skills in addition to reading gauges and dials and also involves a reasonable knowledge of the internal combustion engine.

Conducting a KSA analysis using the focus-group approach can be rather difficult, in that, first, the KSAs are not directly observable and must be inferred by the respondents in the focus group based on their understanding of the job, and, second, the validity of their inferences is a direct function of that understanding. Obviously, the deeper their understanding of the job, the more accurately they will describe the necessary KSAs. This is equally important if we conduct one-on-one interviews rather than group interviews. As with the WAs, once the KSAs for the job are developed and edited, the importance of each KSA needs to be rated for importance on an equivalent following five-point rating scale.

Consider how important this KSA is for fully effective job performance and then rate its importance, using the following scale to make your judgments:

0   This KSA has no role in successful performance of this job.

1   This KSA has only minor or incidental importance for performance of this job.

2   This KSA is desirable and useful for some minor part of this job.

3   This KSA is essential to fully effective performance in either the entire job or some relatively major part of this job.

4   This KSA is very important to fully effective job performance.

5   This KSA is critically important for fully effective performance for this entire job.

Any difficulties inherent in identifying the KSAs involved in a job are most likely a function of the level of the job. For lower-level jobs, the inferences are usually fairly obvious and readily follow the description of the WA. As we move up the organizational hierarchy, however, the WAs become more conceptual, abstract, and complex, and inferring the KSAs is more difficult. Thus it is far more difficult to infer the KSAs involved in developing a strategic plan for an organization than in tuning a car engine. Another important reason for this difficulty is that there are usually several different approaches to performing these complex WAs, and it is rarely clear that one of these approaches is more likely to lead to success or failure.

It should be noted that the relationship between WA and the necessary KSAs is not one-to-one. A specific work activity may require multiple competencies, and a specific competency is often necessary for several different work activities. For example, at the manager/executive level, strategic planning often requires several different competencies such as problem solving, human resource development, oral and written communication, and interpersonal relationships, to identify but a few. On the other hand, competency in oral communications plays an important role in many work activities, including public and community relations, supervision, labor relations, and so on. Thus, except at the most junior levels, there is unlikely to be a simple correspondence between a single WA and a single KSA.

Since KSAs always are inferred from a WA, the two are inextricably intertwined. Specifying the links between the WA and its KSAs, however, is not only desirable but also recommended by the federal government in the *Uniform Guidelines on Employee Selection Procedures* (1978) in order to establish the validity of the selection process. Such a linkage also provides a clearer specification of the requisite training and development requirements for that WA.

Collecting Job Performance Data

In addition to developing WAs and their KSAs, we also need information on job performance, that is, information on the range of performance on this job. When we conduct individual assessments to fill a job vacancy, we always wish to select candidates who will become high performers, for example, assemblers who will produce the most widgets on their shift or sales representatives who will produce the highest volume of sales or those workers who simply show up regularly and on time. Job performance data allow us to identify incumbent high performers and study them in order to identify those KSAs that are involved in their approach to the job. In other words, what separates these high performers from the rest of the pack?

For some jobs, data on individual job performance is readily available, such as sales data, but ordinarily such data needs be developed as part of the job analysis. This usually requires that the organization begin to collect individual data of job performance systematically, focusing on identifying those elements of job performance that are regarded as most important to organizational success and those that raise organizational problems if they are present. These elements, sometimes known as *critical incidents*, are necessary to clearly separate behaviors at both ends of the job-performance continuum. This is a time-consuming and labor-intensive process, but is an important one that allows the organization to evaluate the worth of the assessment process (Flanagan, 1954).

A somewhat easier and relatively direct way to collect such performance data is through benchmarking. Ask supervisors and managers to identify the two or three best performers on a job and then study their behavior as compared to a small number of average performers and a similar number of poor performers. Benchmarking is a time-honored procedure that facilitates our understanding of those performance behaviors that differentiate various levels of job performance. Such data (see page 78 in Chapter Four), in fact, illustrate the linkage between WAs and KSAs and provide insight into on-the-job performance. Highly effective performers will usually demonstrate higher levels of KSAs on those WAs ranked "4" or "5," very or most important and essential to effective job performance. The data on poor performers is especially useful in identifying WAs that are either not being carried out or are being executed incorrectly.

The most important use of job performance data, however, is to provide the criteria for validation studies of the assessment process. In order to validate an assessment process, we would correlate our assessment data with subsequent job performance. The output(s) from a valid assessment process should be well correlated with job performance; otherwise, they are suspect at best!

Collecting Data on Work-Setting Characteristics

Not all workplaces are created equal. Each workplace has its own culture—its unwritten rules and ways of executing its functions. While we are not suggesting that a competent job analysis requires the input of a cultural anthropologist, the most important elements of the culture of this workplace need to be identified and included in the job analysis. For example, organizations differ on a variety of cultural dimensions, such as the degree of conformity, autonomy, rewards, communication style, and so on.

We are not suggesting that the job analysis include a complete analysis of the characteristics of the work setting. Rather, those elements that are readily observable and rather distinctive need to be noted. For example, some years ago one of our clients quit his job in a huff when his supervisor objected to his wearing gray socks rather than the required black socks. Such a high degree of required conformity certainly needs to be noted in any job analysis.

The source of this cultural data is the employees of the organization, and it usually can readily be obtained through an interview. Among our favorite questions for eliciting this information are, "If a really good friend of yours were coming to work here, what three things would you tell that person he or she needed to do to succeed here?" and "What are two or three things that he or she might do that are almost certain to get this person into trouble?" Integrating such information into the job analysis will go a long way to improve the selection process in that individuals who do not fit this cultural template over time will not be included in the final candidate pool.

Assembling and Applying the Final Job Analysis

The final job analysis consists of a comprehensive set of WA and KSA statements that can be assembled by arranging the items in subsets according to themes, such as planning, communications, organizing, and so on. Under each category, the WAs that characterize this specific job would be listed in order of importance, using the previously presented five-point rating scale. A listing of the KSAs necessary to perform that work activity, which also had been rated on the previously presented five-point rating scale, follows each WA. This final job analysis provides the specification of the competencies necessary to work successfully at this job. A detailed example of a final job analysis for a supervisor/first-line manager position with seven themes appears in Appendix D.

Once we have specified the necessary competencies to perform the most important work activities, we can then move ahead with the process of conducting the individual assessments to fill this job and rate each candidate on the degree to which he or she possesses the necessary competencies. Applicants should be rated on each KSA using the following five-point scale, which parallels those for rating the importance of WAs and KSAs:

0   This indicates no functional competence in this area.

1   This indicates a limited competence in this area. An individual would have marginal proficiency in the area, but insufficient for employment.

2   This level indicates borderline competency. An individual can work at this job, but some deficiencies in performance would be expected.

3   This level indicates adequate competency in the defined area. "Adequate" indicates sufficient competence for functioning in this job.

4   This level indicates an advanced level of this competency. At this level, the individual would be considered to have journeyman-level competence and should function in an independent and unsupervised way.

5   This level indicates a mastery or superior level of this competency. Such individuals would be considered models for other employees and as an organization resource.

Each KSA is rated separately in order to sharpen the assessment process by focusing on a specific detail. The final overall rating, however, is not the simple average of the individual KSA ratings but rather a global one that takes into account all the available data.

Appendix D

First-Line Management/Supervisory Level Competency Model

It is important to understand that the job title often has only the loosest connection to the actual WA and KSAs. Job titles are often a function of organizational culture and politics and, in developing an in-depth understanding of both WA and KSAs, care should be exercised not to be misled by the title of the job.

When deriving KSAs for a specific WA, it is important to concentrate on identifying the critical knowledge, skills, and abilities necessary for performing that function. We should always use the criterion of whether or not this job could be performed without having this bit of knowledge, this skill or ability. Then in the job analysis report, it is customary to list the WAs in order of importance with the necessary KSA(s) in a similar order.

However, as we noted in Appendix C, there is rarely a one-to-one correspondence between WA and KSAs, especially once we get beyond entry-level positions. Thus, while in the following example of our model the relationships between WA and KSA are relatively transparent, this is not always the case.

First-Line Management/Supervisory Level Work Activities

1. *Management of Performance Quality:* Involves observation and evaluation of an employee's job performance and the application of specific remedies to overcome performance deficiencies. Instruction and training are included in the

remedies by which a supervisor may correct performance deficits.

2. *Staffing/Personnel Actions:* Includes activities that are related to the assignment of employees to specific job duties, assessment of individual capabilities, specification of task requirements, scheduling of action steps, monitoring of task status to adjust assignments or schedules, and enforcing adherence to company policies and procedures.

3. *Communications:* Involves the communication occurring between management and employees during planning and implementation of job assignments, including exchanging information with people concerning objectives, seeking their cooperation, and informing other departments about programs and progress.

4. *Interpersonal Relations:* This performance area is not limited to specific task content but is related to organizational functioning and goals. This area is concerned with effectiveness in creating and maintaining the interpersonal relationships required to conduct work or business activities.

5. *Problem Analysis/Resolution:* Includes the activities involved in analyzing and resolving problems that occur in business situations. Included are specific tasks relating to the investigation and interpretation of information, the development of possible solutions, and the evaluation, choice, and implementation of solutions.

6. *Project Planning:* Includes tasks relating to the detailed scheduling of work activities to accomplish assigned objectives. Project planning involves planning, scheduling, and assigning work activities and monitoring the performance of assigned personnel.

7. *Direct Supervision:* Includes the assignment of personnel to specific tasks and observation of performance, including providing

detailed instruction on work performance, evaluation of work performance, and training in task accomplishment to facilitate close and continuous contact between the supervisor and the employee.

First-Line Management/Supervisory Level Competency Specifications

1. Performance Management
   - Ability to distinguish between effective and ineffective procedures or job performance.
   - Ability to communicate evaluative judgments and descriptive comments on the job performance of subordinates.
   - Knowledge of alternative techniques and procedures for training and their relative advantages or disadvantages.
   - Ability to coach subordinates to correct ineffective work practices or to remedy performance deficiencies.
2. Employee Relations
   - Ability to assess the morale of subordinates.
   - Ability to enforce rules and regulations without alienating others.
   - Ability to apply personnel rules in a fair and consistent manner.
   - Ability to assess the capabilities and limitations of individuals in order to allocate personnel or make job assignments.
3. Communications
   - Skill in soliciting information through interviews or conversation.
   - Ability to convey information in a concise fashion without losing necessary detail.

- Ability to assist others to clarify a request, question, or response that is not clear.
- Ability to translate informal conversation into action-oriented memoranda.

4. Interpersonal Skills

- Skill in the application of timing, tact, and discretion in communicating business-related information.
- Ability to recognize interpersonal problems that interfere with workgroup performance.
- Ability to recognize and capitalize on social and interpersonal cues in dealing with others.
- Ability to focus attention on work assignments or responsibilities in a distracting environment.

5. Ability to Organize and Use Information

- Skill in identifying the relevant facts underlying conflicting claims.
- Ability to take various points of view in analyzing, interpreting, and evaluating data.
- Ability to evaluate and choose between conflicting alternatives based on partial or incomplete information.
- Ability to locate and identify primary and/or contributory causes of equipment or manufacturing problems.

6. Ability to Schedule and Orchestrate People and Activities

- Knowledge of factors that have an effect on work assignment completion time.
- Ability to coordinate the activities of other individuals or departments on joint projects.
- Ability to schedule multiple projects that compete for limited resources (time, equipment, personnel, etc.).
- Ability to evaluate and to establish project priorities based on relative merits, demands, or requirements.

7. Direct Supervision

- Ability to recognize and capitalize on situational restrictions or conditions that affect choice of supervisory style.

- Ability to recognize and deal with conditions that interfere with the performance of employees.

- Ability to react immediately and give precise instructions in emergency situations.

- Ability to assign tasks and delegate authority in relation to a subordinate's capabilities and developmental needs.

Appendix E

Senior Management/Executive Level Competency Model

It is important to understand that the job title often has only the loosest connection to the actual WAs and KSAs. Job titles are often a function of organizational culture and politics and, in developing an in-depth understanding of both WAs and KSAs, care should be exercised not to be misled by the title of the job.

When deriving KSAs for a specific WA, it is important to concentrate on identifying the critical knowledge, skills, and abilities necessary for performing that function. We should always use the criterion of whether or not this job could be performed without having this bit of knowledge, this skill or ability. Then in the job analysis report, it is customary to list the WAs in order of importance with the necessary KSA(s) in a similar order.

However, as we noted in Appendix C, there is rarely a one-to-one correspondence between WA and KSAs, especially once we go beyond entry-level positions. Thus, while in the following example of our model the relationships between WA and KSA are relatively transparent, this is not always the case.

Management/Executive Level Work Activities

1. *Schedule and Orchestrate Business and Activities:* Develop limited or short-term business plans or activities in order to keep business operations moving smoothly.

2. *Public and Community Relations:* Manage and participate in the relationship between the organization and the general public

and community. Represent the organization to the public and community agencies both directly and indirectly through activities such as speeches, conferences, and press releases.

3. *Management Control of Work Operations and Products:* Monitor the work process and products to keep informed and to ensure standards and objectives are being met.

4. *Financial Management:* Prepare and justify budgets, monitor financial and economic information, and maintain management control of the utilization of financial resources.

5. *Strategic Planning:* Formulate long-range business plans and strategic philosophy; set organizational goals and develop strategies for meeting those goals; anticipate possible problems and prepare contingent strategies; and analyze industry trends to identify potential business opportunities.

6. *Human Resource Management:* Manage and participate in the development of the organization's human resources for business purposes. Evaluate employee performance and business requirements to identify training needs and develop programs to facilitate the acquisition of job-related knowledge, skills, and abilities.

7. *Employee-Oriented Supervision:* Direct the activities of individuals and groups toward the accomplishment of work and organizational goals. Monitor performance and clarify work expectations, motivate subordinates, and promote cooperation among individuals and groups.

8. *Sales and Marketing Management:* Monitor and manage the linkage between the organization's products or services and customers or potential customers. Evaluate customer and prospect potential; prepare sales proposals; develop ideas for advertising and direct sales efforts.

9. *Internal Consulting:* Work with other people in the organization on an "as needed" basis to help define and solve problems. Give

professional advice and specialized assistance on problems and provide others with facts or information.

10. *Labor Relations:* Review and manage the organization's relations with employees either individually or collectively. Develop and maintain relations with employees or bargaining groups; review labor contract proposals; examine details of agreements; and provide advice and counsel concerning the handling of grievances.

11. *Facilities Operations Management:* Observe and inspect installations, buildings, equipment, and facilities for the purpose of determining operating conditions; evaluate plant sites; and review plans for plant construction.

12. *Personnel Administration:* Manage or administer existing organizational policies and procedures involving personnel, including recruitment, selection, compensation, and benefits, and relevant reports and records.

13. *Monitor Operations for Regulatory Compliance:* Monitor and evaluate business objectives, requirements, and operations in terms of external constraints in the form of standards and regulations. Review and interpret government directives or bulletins for applicability to the organization and represent company interests before legal authorities.

14. *Management Information Systems:* Analyze and interpret data using computers and packaged software programs. Match computer capabilities and software with organizational requirements and determine what kind of system information is required.

15. *Materials Management:* Ensure effectiveness and efficiency in the use of organization resources.

16. *Safety:* Inspect the work setting and work process for potential safety and health hazards, monitor compliance with safety regulations, and instruct workers in safe working habits.

Management/Executive Level Competency Specifications

1. Problem Solving

   - Ability to recognize when and to specify what additional information should be collected to facilitate problem solving.'

   - Ability to evaluate data from multiple sources and integrate it to formulate recommendations.

   - Ability to adapt data-gathering approaches for problem solving to best fit various conditions and constraints.

   - Ability to determine the point at which a deviation from expectancy becomes significant and constitutes a problem.

2. Schedule and Orchestrate Business Activities

   - Ability to determine proper priority and perspective when handling multiple activities or projects.

   - Ability to determine when, where, and how to establish and maintain management controls to monitor individual or team activities.

   - Ability to calculate manpower, materials, and other resource requirements for completion of activities or projects.

   - Ability to determine the sequence in which component parts or steps of a project or activity must be conducted.

3. Human Resource Development

   - Ability to counsel staff on their training and development needs in order to help them attain their career goals.

   - Ability to identify a person's strengths and weaknesses in relation to job performance.

   - Ability to design training and development programs to meet the requirements established in training needs assessment.

4. Long-Range Planning

   - Ability to formulate long-range program plans to address significant issues or goals, using systematic methods, such as PERT or CPM.

- Ability to identify the key decision points and milestones in the planning, implementation, and control of a project.
- Knowledge of the significant factors to be considered and how to weight them when making strategic organizational decisions.
- Knowledge of activities of competitors and trends within the area of business that could create future opportunities or problems.

5. Oral Communications

- Ability to phrase and sequence questions to obtain information or clarify issues through interviews and/or informal conversations.
- Ability to summarize the comments, observations, and opinions of others.
- Ability to design a presentation that addresses the interests of the listeners and takes into account their level of understanding.

6. Sales and Marketing Management

- Ability to analyze existing accounts or client relationships to determine the potential for further development.
- Ability to conceive and develop advertising campaigns to achieve goals.
- Ability to determine what constitutes desirable characteristics of possible customers, clients, or markets to guide sales representatives' efforts at prospecting and qualifying.
- Ability to develop new or modified products and services based on inferred or developing changes in customer interests and needs.

7. Employee-Oriented Supervision

- Ability to disregard one's personal feelings in the assignment of tasks or in the conduct of business activities.
- Ability to explain or demonstrate work techniques to subordinates and provide feedback on their performance.

- Ability to evaluate the performance of subordinates in terms of organizational requirements and standards.
- Ability to recognize situational constraints or conditions that affect choice of supervisory behavior or style.

8. Public Relations

- Ability to identify key members of the community who represent different constituencies and who can influence the outcome of opinions.
- Ability to develop and maintain sources of information in the community, concerning the image of the organization.
- Knowledge of the social protocols involved in conducting special events and employee activities.
- Skill in identifying topics, issues, or concerns about which there is potential conflict between the organization's activities and different community or advocacy groups.

9. Interpersonal Relations

- Ability to ignore personal likes and dislikes in business dealings and focus on the desired outcome of transactions.
- Ability to recognize social and interpersonal cues in dealing with others and to utilize them to realize business purposes.
- Ability to build and maintain credibility in business relations.
- Ability to provide criticism or objections to the views of another in a way that avoids personal accusations or acrimony.

10. Crisis Management

- Ability to adjust one's pace of activity to keep up with rapidly occurring events or changing conditions and circumstances and fulfill the essence of management requirements.
- Ability to identify and prioritize requirements of ongoing operations or projects in order to achieve the desired outcomes.

- Skill in selecting standard solutions to problems or modifying standard operating procedures to make things work when unanticipated, novel, or unique developments occur.
- Ability to identify obstacles to the flow of an activity and to identify and initiate alternative procedures to maintain continuity of the activity.

11. Facilities Planning

- Ability to design appropriate floor plans of physical plants for purposes of fire control, safety, and security.
- Knowledge of standard security and loss-prevention programs.
- Knowledge of maintenance requirements of different building units.
- Knowledge of routine and preventive maintenance required to maintain the operational status of business equipment.

12. Financial Management and Budgeting

- Ability to translate objectives into required activities and identify cost requirements for labor, services, supplies, and equipment in order to develop a budget.
- Knowledge of how accounting/financial information should be arranged for various management uses.
- Ability to analyze financial statements to locate the causes of variances in business operations.
- Ability to gather information obtained from economic indicators, trends, and business cycles, and to interpret such information for use in forecasting.

13. Staffing

- Knowledge of the relevant labor market and sources for recruiting potential employees for different labor/professional classifications.
- Knowledge of federal, state, and local laws or guidelines concerning employee benefits packages.

- Ability to identify relevant applicant background and characteristics through reviews of resumes, application blanks, etc.

- Ability to identify issues that have a significant impact on employee welfare and morale.

- Knowledge of federal, state, and local laws or regulations regarding employment practices and personnel actions.

14. Written Communications

- Ability to review reports for quality using standards of logic, clarity, and adequacy of recommendations and supporting arguments.

- Ability to prepare technical reports for use by others with comparable background.

- Ability to communicate company policy or intent in contracts, letters, or other formal documents.

- Ability to prepare clear instructions or delegations in written format.

Sample Individual Assessment Report on Applicant for Administrative Assistant Position

Confidential Memorandum

To: Steven R. Minders
           Executive Vice President
           b2bPartners.com

From: Jodie R. Smith
           HR Specialist

Date: September 20, 2005

Re: Christina Walker
           Administrative Assistant Candidate

I. Identifying Information

This report summarizes the results of the screening assessment of Christina Walker, a candidate for a position as Administrative Assistant with b2bPartners.com.

    Ms. Walker is a 42-year-old high school graduate with five years' experience as a file clerk in a local employment agency. Prior to that employment, she was a stay-at-home mother for several years. She arrived promptly for her appointment and she comes across as a pleasant person, one eager to please but not overly so. She was well-dressed and carefully groomed and overall made a positive impression on me and the others at the office.

In addition to a 25-minute behavioral interview, Ms. Walker was administered the following tests:

Advanced Mental Abilities Test, Short Form
Arithmetic Reasoning Test
Business Relations Skills Test
Gordon Personal Profile
Planning and Organizing Skills Test
Teamwork and Organization Skills Test
Work Readiness and Adaptability Profile

This individual assessment was conducted by me at the offices of b2b Partners.com without incident.

II. Functional Analysis and Person/Job Fit

A. Personal/Interpersonal Functioning. Ms. Walker is a very self-sufficient individual who has little interest in socializing with other people. She, however, does interact with other people as necessary to get her work done, and she has a good understanding of appropriate behavior in the business setting. Ms. Walker is extremely pleasant and easy to get along with, but she prefers to work alone rather than as a team member. When she encounters resistance or has conflicts with associates, she prefers to give in and accommodate other people. Her associates and contacts have generally viewed Ms. Walker as being very business-like, helpful, and calm, and there is no reason to doubt that this will continue to be the case.
Rating 4

B. Intellectual Functioning. Ms. Walker has a superior level of cognitive ability as compared to the non-exempt office and clerical population. Her job-related skills of reasoning and problem solving are quite well-developed and she usually "works smart" and will quickly learn what is required to complete a task. Ms. Walker does

tend to stick with solutions she knows when solving problems, rather than trying out alternatives. It is not that she lacks confidence in her ability, but rather she prefers to use the methods that she knows will get the work done. Finally, Ms. Walker will stick to her assignment and will persist until she finds the answer to a problem.
Rating 4

C. Scheduling and Coordinating Skills. Ms. Walker has superior knowledge of planning and organizing activities, even in comparison to a supervisory and managerial population. She very efficiently organizes her time and sets her priorities without needing assistance from her supervisor. Ms. Walker will carry out her routine or schedule in a very calm, deliberate manner, completing tasks one at a time in an orderly progression. Ms. Walker does not like to have her plans disrupted or changed; however, if she is asked to do so, she does comply willingly and calmly.
Rating 5

D. Work Motivation and Adaptation. Ms. Walker is a very conscientious person and has a compelling sense of personal responsibility as well as a strong goal orientation. She adapts readily to necessary changes in the workplace, although she prefers not to have her own schedule disrupted. Ms. Walker will be the model of a good organizational citizen and will get along quite well with her co-workers. However, Ms. Walker is fairly introverted and should not be expected to take a leadership role or participate in social activities. Others, however, will regard her as quite capable, agreeable, and non-threatening.
Rating 4

E. Arithmetic Skills. Ms. Walker has superior ability to work with numbers. Her work style is generally detail-oriented and persistent, and she will check her work until she is sure that she has the right answer. In working with numbers, Ms. Walker prefers to use the methods with which she is familiar, as she believes that this will

ensure that she is getting the right answer. When necessary, however, she is able to learn new methods of working with numbers.
Rating 5

III. *Conclusions and Recommendations*

Both the interview and test data provide good evidence that Ms. Walker possesses the necessary competencies to performance successfully as an administrative assistant at b2b Partners.

The results of this assessment provide strong support for a positive recommendation of Ms. Christina Walker to be hired for this position.

Her final rating of suitability for this position is 4.

Sample Assessment Report— Supervisor/First-Line Manager

Confidential Assessment Report on Roger Martin

Prepared for Barnes Stores
3501 S. Saguaro Shadows
Tucson, AZ 85730
By John Peter Long, M.A.
April 14, 2006

I. Identifying Information

This report summarizes the results of an individual assessment of Roger Martin, which was conducted on April 10, 2006. The purpose for the assessment was to determine Mr. Martin's suitability for employment in a Department Manager Trainee position as well as his potential to develop into a Department Manager for the Barnes Stores of Arizona. Clyde Barnes, Senior Vice President of Barnes Stores, authorized this assessment.

Mr. Martin is a 32-year-old high school graduate with two years of college. He is tall, thin, and appears younger than others his age. He came casually dressed for the assessment, but not exceptionally inappropriately. His approach to the assessment process varies from casual to disinterested and he comes across as having a chip on his shoulder. His work history consists mainly of short-term jobs in fast-food restaurants, seasonal work in the building trades as a helper, and some seasonal work in two small retail stores.

In addition to a one-hour behavioral interview, Mr. Martin was administered the following tests:

Advanced Mental Abilities Test—Long Form

Arithmetic Reasoning Test

Business Relations Skills Test

Customer Relations Test

Gordon Personal Profile/Inventory

Leadership Opinion Questionnaire

Mechanical Understanding Skills Test

Numerical Computational Test

Planning and Organizing Skills Test

Sales Ability Test

Test of Supervisory Skills

Work Readiness and Adaptability Profile

Although Mr. Martin was skeptical of the assessment process, there was no indication that he was uncooperative or careless in responding to the tests. Thus, the results reported below can be assumed to be valid.

Following completion of the assessment, the results were discussed with Mr. Martin, emphasizing both his strengths and weaknesses in filling this position and providing him with an opportunity to discuss his results. Mr. Martin indicted that he had taken the Fire Department Entry Examination on six different occasions but had never been hired and is thus very skeptical about testing. This latter comment was offered in a rather hostile manner, an issue that was brought to his attention. In the later discussion, he noted that his tendency to be outspoken had cost him at least one of his previous jobs. After some further discussion, he indicated that he was quite satisfied with the test results and confirmed the accuracy of the feedback.

This report contains three additional sections. The first describes Mr. Martin's functioning in the three general areas: Personal/Interpersonal; Intellectual; and Work Motivation. The next section reports on how well Mr. Martin fits the requirements for success on this job with Barnes Stores. This section consists of short evaluative statements covering the seven different competencies, together with a numerical rating. The final section consists of conclusions and recommendations.

II. Functional Analysis

A. Personal/Interpersonal Characteristics. The results of the assessment indicate that Mr. Martin is not a very social person and that he is very assertive and tends to be rather outspoken. He is quite comfortable working alone, although when he is with his peers, he can be quite congenial. Mr. Martin is not interested in social leadership and, although he is quite articulate, shows little interest in persuading people or in having social influence with them. People who know him describe him as an introverted, quiet person who prefers to work at those things that personally interest him.

At work, Mr. Martin tends to stick to business and avoid socializing with colleagues and customers. At the same time, he also feels free to express his opinions to others, often to their dismay. Since he is not inhibited about what he says, he will often rub people the wrong way. While he does know what people expect in the business setting, he often does not use that information to influence what he will say or do. Mr. Martin is an individual with unusual personal values and attitudes that influence his performance in work and social settings. For example, he wants to be independent and not be held to traditional social standards. While he does recognize that to survive it is necessary to accommodate and conform in order to fulfill his job responsibilities, he often finds this difficult to accomplish.

B. Intellectual Functioning. The assessment reveals that Mr. Martin has above average intellectual abilities in comparison with the general population. He does not use his intellect except where it is necessary to achieve his own specific goals. As a result, he has not developed a uniform level of job skills commensurate with his level of cognitive functioning. For example, his skill in handling numerical computations is superior, but his knowledge of sales skills and of good supervisory practices is at the bottom of the distribution.

In reviewing Mr. Martin's work history, it is clear that, as he has bounced from job to job, he did learn something in almost every case. He is somewhat well informed and has not been unwilling to learn, but, for one reason or another, he simply has not developed adequate understanding of how things work in the world of work—there are just too many blind spots.

C. Work Motivation.   Mr. Martin shows many of the characteristics of an adolescent free spirit who wants to be independent, unrestricted, undisciplined, and accountable only to himself. When he works, it is important to him that he have a personal sense of accomplishment and competence, but conventional aspects of achievement, for example, recognition, advancement, and bonuses, are relatively unimportant to him. In terms of his work motivation, Mr. Martin is not a very mature individual and, while he has good insight to his personal motivation, he does not adapt readily to either work or organization requirements. Mr. Martin is under some pressure at the present time from his wife to either get a job or get out of their home, and thus he is seeking full-time employment.

III. Person/Job Fit

A. Performance Management.   The assessment indicates that Mr. Martin has an action-oriented and task-oriented style of leadership, a strong sense of personal responsibility, and a high level of energy and initiative. In the work setting, he will establish priorities and provide individuals with feedback that may at times be blunt and direct, but will, nonetheless, result in productivity.
Rating 4

B. Employee Relations Activities. Mr. Martin will be a supervisor who will try to get along with those he supervises. He has good knowledge of what people expect in the work setting and can be generally accommodating except when he expresses his thoughts or opinions in a direct or outspoken way. Mr. Martin simply does not know when to keep his mouth shut or use tact in order to maintain a harmonious relation. In addition, he lacks knowledge and understanding of good supervisory practices so that, while he is willing to assert himself and try to solve supervisory problems, he frequently does not know what to do.
Rating 3

C. Customer Relations and Communications. Mr. Martin has a very adequate vocabulary and can express his thoughts clearly, but he tends to be rather reserved, rarely initiating an interaction with others. While he has good knowledge of the business setting, he has extremely limited knowledge of sales techniques and skills. As a result, he will do what comes naturally to him, which may or may not be appropriate for contact with customers.
Rating 2

D. Interpersonal Skills. Mr. Martin is an assertive individual who speaks his mind and will do so when he often should be quiet. He has good knowledge of what is expected in a business setting and, when necessary, will use that knowledge to get along with others, but not in a persuasive or influential fashion.
Rating 3

E. Problem Analysis. Mr. Martin has average abilities in comparison with the population of supervisors and has developed a mixed array of problem-analysis skills. If something is important to him, he will develop some analytic competency in that area; if it is not important to him, he ignores it. As a result, he has very limited knowledge of good supervisory practices or of sales skills, but excellent computational skills and good planning and organizing skills.

He does have the potential to analyze and solve supervisory problems and to develop the necessary competencies, but only if he becomes interested in doing so.
Rating 4

F. Scheduling and Orchestrating People and Activities. Mr. Martin has average knowledge of planning and organizing operations, but he is a very energetic individual with a very strong sense of personal responsibility. He is very decisive and has a high level of initiative, but what he actually does will depend on his personal interests and motivations rather than the needs of the organization. While the ability to schedule and implement plans is present, this ability may not be implemented.
Rating 3

G. Direct Supervision. Mr. Martin has a relatively action-oriented style of leadership, which places considerably stronger emphasis on working with people and being considerate of others, except when his "hot buttons" are pushed. He will also get along very well with peers by doing what comes naturally but may have more problems with those he supervises. His interest in supervisory functions and his attitudes toward any organizational hierarchy are certainly less than optimal for this or any supervisory role. In addition, he has very limited knowledge of good supervisory practices.
Rating 3

IV. Conclusions and Recommendation

While Mr. Martin does appear to have many of the competencies required to satisfactorily fill the job as a management trainee, the many problems caused by his personal/interpersonal style make it unlikely that he can function effectively in this trainee job, at least not in the long run.

While the results of this assessment offer some support for a positive recommendation of Mr. Martin, his lack of a strong work motivation and personal maturity inevitably lead to the conclusion that he is a poor risk for long-term employment. Mr. Martin may be at a turning point in his life, but at the present time the most likely prediction is that he will continue to function as he has in the past, that is, bounce from one job to another, while asserting his independence and freedom to act as he sees fit.

Overall Rating 2

Appendix H

Sample Individual Assessment Report—Management and Executive Level

Confidential Assessment Report on Michael Z. Clement

Prepared for Fred G. Williams, Vice President, Human Resources, Atlantic Apparel Corporation, P.O. Box 570, Wabash, IN 46992
By Julius B. Strong, Ph.D., Consulting Psychologist
May 12, 2006

This Confidential Assessment Report is intended for use by client-authorized management personnel only. Statements by the author are based on professional interpretation of interviews, biographical information, psychological tests, and the requirements and standards of the client organization. Such statements would be of limited use to the individual and could be misleading to parties other than the client.

I. Identifying Information

This report summarizes the results of an individual assessment of Michael (Mike) Z. Clement, conducted on May 8, 2006, in our Memphis office. The purpose of the assessment was to evaluate Mr. Clement as a candidate for the position of president of the Ladies and Girls Division of the Atlantic Apparel Corporation.

Mr. Clement is a 35-year-old graduate of Florida State University with a major in business. He is of average height with a stocky build. Since graduating from college he has held a series of jobs of increasing responsibility in the ladies garment industry. Until January of 2006, he was employed as executive vice president of Ranger Fashions in Dallas, Texas. Ranger was acquired by a competitor at that time and Mr. Clement was terminated. Since January, he has been actively seeking employment.

On his arrival, the purpose for the assessment and its schedule were explained to Mr. Clement. He expressed surprise that the process would take the entire day; he commented that he had expected an hour or two would be sufficient for the testing and interviewing, which is what he had experienced in prior pre-employment situations. However, he did not object to staying the full day and worked diligently on all of the materials. There was, however, a consistent and continuous low-level expression of skepticism, irritation, and impatience with the initial process.

In an effort to engage Mr. Clement more fully in the assessment process, he was moved into a larger, more private office with outside windows, and the sequence of testing was changed in order to confront him with some immediate significant challenge. These changes appeared to have the intended effect. Mr. Clement and I had a long lunch together and then returned to complete the testing and to begin the interview. The completion of the testing, the interview, and the subsequent feedback continued until it was time for him to go to the airport to return home to Dallas.

In addition to a 75-minute behavioral interview, Mr. Clement was administered the following tests:

Advanced Mental Abilities Test—Long Form*

Arithmetic Reasoning Test

Business Relations Skills Test

Customer Relations Skills Test

Gordon Personal Profile/Inventory

Leadership Opinion Questionnaire

Management and Organizational Skills

Mechanical Understanding Skills Test*

Numerical Computational Test*

Planning and Organizing Skills Test

Sales Ability Test

Test of Supervisory Skills

Teamwork and Organization Skills Test

Watson-Glaser Critical Thinking Appraisal*

Work Readiness and Adaptability Profile

This report contains three additional sections. The first describes Mr. Clement's functioning in the three general areas: Personal/ Interpersonal; Intellectual; and Work Motivation. The next section reports on how well Mr. Clement fits the requirements for success on this job with Atlantic Apparel. This section consists of short evaluative statements covering the ten different competencies, together with a numerical rating. This set of competency specifications was derived from the job analysis prepared by Mr. Fred Williams, vice president for Human Resources of Atlantic Apparel. The final section consists of conclusions and recommendations.

II. Functional Analysis

A. Personal/Interpersonal Functioning. The results of the assessment, including the testing data, observations, interviews, and discussions with Mr. Clement, clearly indicate that he is a spontaneous, very talkative, and socially dynamic person. He is quite uninhibited, constantly and energetically establishing and maintaining relations with others for either business or social reasons. He is not comfortable with constraints on his style and some people will be not comfortable with him, as they will view him as being too assertive, opportunistic, and perhaps even a bit self-serving.

---

*These tests were administered twice because Mr. Clement's scores were lower than would be expected of someone with his education and work experience. However, there were no significant changes on retesting.

When he does alienate others in his interpersonal relations and receives feedback about his behavior, he is quite responsive to this feedback and makes efforts to modify his behavior and heal the breach. Unfortunately, however, his social sensitivity is barely adequate, which means that he often finds himself having alienated someone. His strong motivation to establish and maintain relations is extraordinarily high so that he spends considerable effort making amends for his prior acts. There is little doubt that Mr. Clement is a very people-oriented person and that this orientation is a basic aspect of his success as a person and a manager.

In the work setting, Mr. Clement will be a fairly continuous source of stimulation to other people. He will be continually planning, coordinating, facilitating the work of others, but sometimes manipulating and irritating them on an equally continuous basis. For those individuals who accept and share his goals for the organization, these are minor irritations that will be seen as incidental and easily overlooked. Those individuals who do not share his vision or accept his goals, however, will undoubtedly be uncomfortable working with him and will probably leave sooner or later. This will occur not because he has ignored them, but rather because of his continual efforts to bring them into his team. Mr. Clement has a very action-oriented leadership style, backed by superior knowledge of good supervisory practices and an array of job-related skills that enhance his effectiveness as a leader of others and a facilitator of work.

B. Intellectual Functioning. The assessment results indicate that Mr. Clement has a low-average level of cognitive ability in comparison to other senior managers and executives. He is continuously alert and, when he confronts very complex or abstract problems or issues, he focuses his attention on these problems, fully confident that he can master the material and eventually solve the problem. Because of his intellectual limitations, Mr. Clement tends to rely on trial-and-error for solving problems, but over his career, he has developed a strategy of surrounding himself with the best talent available and using it liberally to resolve difficult situations.

During the assessment, he recognized that the limits of his intelligence were being challenged and worked exceptionally hard to try to improve his performance, but to little avail. During the feedback session, his total attention was focused on the data and its meaning for his personal future. He recognizes and accepts that he has some limitations as a person but strongly believes that hard work and personal charm can make up for these limitations.

Mr. Clement is a very inquisitive individual, very flexible and spontaneous, with a high level of ideational fluency. This means that he will be very uninhibited in coming up with ideas, which is integral to his problem-solving strategy. He has come to believe in applying effort and energy toward solving a problem until he comes on a solution or one of his colleagues or subordinates offers a more elegant solution.

Mr. Clement has developed an impressive array of job-related management skills for day-to-day operations and on the available standardized tests of such skills, his scores are in the superior range. In a lengthy, probing interview he demonstrated a high degree of expertise, interpersonal competency, and self-confidence. He views himself as a natural-born salesman, merchant, and sales executive. His high level of pragmatic skills suggests that he has superior *tacit knowledge*. People who possess tacit knowledge naturally seem to do things right, even though they are unable to explain why or how they arrived at a course of action.

C. Work Motivation. Mr. Clement is an extremely achievement-oriented individual who dedicates his effort and energy to goal accomplishment without reservation or restrictions. He is a man with a mission, who sooner or later finds a place for executing that mission and then focuses his attention and energy to achieving practical goals. Mr. Clement needs to experience a sense of achievement and accomplishment and he wants to leave work each day feeling that important things have been accomplished.

Mr. Clement is quite restless and does not sit still very long. He will be very effective in inspiring and motivating the people around him and in getting work done. He thrives in the dynamic and volatile business environment of the apparel industry and continuously looks for the excitement furnished by the industry.

The assessment results indicate that Mr. Clement is well-adjusted and has adequate self-awareness. He accepts himself and his limitations and tends to capitalize on his strengths in order to enjoy a very rich and full life. While he is brash and sometimes abrasive, he is not without awareness of these tendencies. There are no indications that his motives, values, or attitudes would lead to actions that would harm other people or his organization. He does have a strong sense of propriety and ethics and will work to establish and maintain such a climate in his organization.

III. Person/Job Fit

A. Problem Solving. The results of the assessment indicate that Mr. Clement has low average problem-solving skills in comparison to his peers, but that he has developed an impressive array of very practical job-related skills that he uses to his advantage in his work. He uses trial and error as his primary problem-solving approach, which frequently works to produce a solution, even though it may not always be an elegant one. When he encounters problems beyond his capacity, he tries to solve such problems by bringing in others with the necessary talent. He has an extremely high level of self-confidence and will not be intimidated by an obstacle or pessimistic thinking on the part of others.

There will be occasions, however, when he will ignore a problem or even gloss over a real problem, dealing with the symptoms of the problem rather than the core problem. This can occur because he is very reactive and intent on pursuing the goal. He is not a highly critical or analytical thinker and often will base decisions on the more obvious aspects of a problem or situation. This is obviously an area of weakness where some mechanisms need to be built into his job to ensure that fundamental, highly complex problems receive the necessary attention.

Rating 2

B. Scheduling, Coordinating, and Orchestrating Operations. Mr. Clement has superior knowledge of coordinating and orchestrating procedures and requirements and his personal and work style will contribute to high levels of organizational effectiveness. He views himself and will be seen by others as the leader of the band, maintaining control of his work environment. On the other hand, he is not detail-oriented but does recognize the need to attention to detail, which he delegates successfully to others.
Rating 5

C. Strategic Planning. Mr. Clement is a strategic thinker and will always be thinking and planning about the medium-term and long-term future of his business. He regularly sets future goals that are appropriate and attractive to others as well as considers plans on how to get there. He will be less effective dealing with the complexity of integrating the various business systems, for example, integrating finances, manufacturing, distribution, sales, and merchandising. While he has an understanding that these various systems must operate as an integrated system, he will not always be able to deal simultaneously with the several components of the system. When he encounters such issues, however, he will use the talent of the team that he has gathered around him. Nevertheless, this is an area in which some job redesign may be necessary in order to compensate for this weakness.
Rating 3

D. Oral Communications. Mr. Clement is a very talkative individual with a very high level of social initiative. He will enter into any social setting, find or make a niche for himself, and then proceed to establish positive relations with others. He has a good vocabulary, but is not always very articulate. He is not purposefully evasive, but there are occasions on which he is not able to meaningfully communicate his thoughts. While he does not lose his main train of thought, he does go off on tangents or provide only partial answers or explanation. Occasionally, he uses talking as a way of avoiding answering question. He certainly does allow interruptions and is appropriately responsive when interrupted. In most settings, his personal and social style of communicating will be reasonably effective and acceptable. For formal presentations, however, it would be very desirable to have him use a script to keep him in bounds. **Rating 3**

E. Sales and Marketing Management. In this area, Mr. Clement had surprisingly average scores on a measure of sales ability. He explained his approach to sales and merchandising as being somewhat unconventional and indicated that the test uses a more conventional orientation. This is a very insightful and probably accurate comment. In his work history Mr. Clement has demonstrated an impressive level of competence in selling and product merchandising. He can be expected to move the company's merchandising effort forward with impressive effectiveness. **Rating 5**

F. Employee-Oriented Supervision. Mr. Clement is a very action-oriented leader with superior knowledge of good supervisory practices. He will be a continuous source of inspiration to those around him. He deals with problem employees and those who have not accepted his goals for the organization by exerting considerable effort to bring them onto his team. He will be quite effective coaching individuals and focusing them on his goals and providing them with the support needed to function effectively. **Rating 4**

G. Interpersonal Relations. Mr. Clement is a very spontaneous and dynamic individual who will work at making everyone else into a collaborator, colleague, or friend. If he does rub someone the wrong way and receives feedback to that effect, he will accommodate and adapt to that individual in order to repair the relationship. He works at establishing harmonious relations with other people, but he will not hesitate to persuade, and if necessary, manipulate. But he always attempts to move people toward the appropriate goals. His style can

be intimidating to some people and irritating to a few, but in the business setting among those people who are goal oriented and see themselves as part of his team, he will be seen as refreshing and inspiring.
Rating 4

H. Crisis Management.   Because of his intense approach to life and work, Mr. Clement is always ready for a crisis. He continually works at maintaining a broad perspective without getting bogged down in details, which allows him to identify and respond promptly to crisis situations. On occasion, he can gloss over a problem or issue, but if it becomes magnified, he will quickly pay attention to it and move to resolve the matter. Mr. Clement is an individual who will benefit from having a very competent executive secretary as well as supporting talent that he can use as resources to keep operations running smoothly. One reservation is that Mr. Clement does not deal with very complex systemic problems as effectively as desired.
Rating 4

I. Written Communications.   Mr. Clement has adequate writing competence and respects the need for documentation. As in his oral communications, however, while he will produce a great deal of content, he does not always get his point across as clearly as he should. While he does not misuse words and does know the mechanics of grammar, he is not always as effective in translating his thoughts into clear and concise writing.
Rating 3

J. Work and Organization Adaptation.   Mr. Clement is quite visionary and is searching for a place to bring his vision about, implementing his goal of heading a business with a sales and marketing focus. He talks about having a variety of other employment opportunities, but not very convincingly. Mr. Clement is an individual who marches to his own drummer, but also wants to be the

band leader who keeps things moving at an ever-accelerating pace. Being in charge is important to him, and he has a strong sense of territoriality coupled with a need to be autonomous. Thus, he does not always welcome intrusions from others he has not personally invited to his party. He is very willing to share the rewards with those whom he regards as part of his team, but needs to be the one handing out the envelopes.
Rating 3

IV. Conclusions and Recommendation

This has been a difficult assessment because Mr. Clement has so many contradictory characteristics. While in many respects he is a very talented, highly competent, and effective person, he has many limitations, some of which are severe. He has only average cognitive ability, limited problem-solving skills, and often has difficulty in clearly expressing himself, both orally and in writing. But he clearly has an impressive track record.

On balance, the results of this assessment support a guarded recommendation of Mr. Clement as a candidate for the position as president of the Ladies and Girls Division with the reservations noted. To compensate for his noted limitations, I recommend that this position be redesigned so that he must collaborate with others in the executive hierarchy to ensure that long-term business plans are implemented and objectives accomplished.
Overall Rating 3+

Appendix I

Selected Tests and Publishers*

---

*It would virtually impossible to list all the psychological tests now commercially available. This list is based on the two primary considerations: first, the use of these tests is supported by considerable empirical research, and second, the authors have found these particular instruments to be helpful to them in their many years of actual practice.

189

I. Tests of Personality and Interest

A. Personality

Test and Test Type	Description	Time	Target Population
1. California Psychological Inventory (CPI)** *Consulting Psychologists Press* [800–624–1765]	Designed to measure three structural scales, twenty "folk scales," and seven special purpose scales	45 minutes (Untimed)	Wide range of adult groups; 8th-grade reading level
2. Gordon Personal Profile Inventory (CPPI) *Psychological Corporation* [800–211–8378]	Designed to measure nine dimensions of personality	25 minutes (Untimed)	Mid- and entry-level mgmt. Supervisor Higher-level administrative
3. Guilford-Zimmerman Temperament Survey (GZTS) *Pearson Assessments* [800–627–7271]	Measures ten dimensions of personality and temperament	50 minutes (Untimed)	Management Supervisor Administrative
4. Hogan Personality Inventory (HPI) *Hogan Assessment Systems* [800–756–0632]	Based on the five-factor approach; provides seven primary scales and six occupational scales	20 minutes (Untimed)	Wide range of adult groups

**Use restricted to doctoral-level professionals.

Test and Test Type	Description	Time	Target Population
5. JobCLUES *Psichometrics, International LLC* [888–477–3883]	Yields five-factor scores plus teamwork and validity scores, plus brief measure of general cognitive ability	20 minutes (Personality test untimed; cognitive test 10 minutes)	Thirty different job families
6. NEO Five Factor Inventory *PAR* [800–331–8378]	A short version of the NEO PI-R, designed to measure the five domains of adult personality	10 to 15 minutes (Untimed)	Wide range of adult groups
7. NEO Pi-R *PAR* [800–331–8378]	The full version of NEO, designed to measure the five domains of adult personality	35 to 45 minutes (Untimed)	Wide range of adult groups
8. 16PF *IPAT* [217–352–9674]	Designed to measure sixteen factorially differentiated personality dimensions	45 minutes (Untimed)	Wide range of adult groups
9. Jackson Personality Test (JPS) *Sigma Assessment Systems* [800–265–1285]	Designed to measure seventeen different dimensions of personality	45 minutes (Untimed)	Wide range of adult groups

B. Tests of Interest

Test and Test Type	Description	Time	Target Population
1. Campbell Interest and Skill Survey (CISS) Pearson Assessments [800–627–7271]	Allows exploration of 299 occupations and 159 fields of study	25 minutes (Untimed)	Wide range of occupations
2. Motives, Values Preferences Inventory (MVPI) Hogan Assessment Systems [800–756–0632]	Designed to measure ten motives and their underlying values	15 to 20 minutes (Untimed)	Late adolescents and adults
3. Kuder Occupation Interest Survey (KOIS) National Career Assessment Services [800–314–8972]	Designed to measure eleven broad interest areas. Compares scores with 119 occupations	40 minutes (Untimed)	Late adolescents and adults
4. Self-Directed Search (SDS) PAR [800–331–8378]	Measures seven career interests based on Holland's typology	35 to 45 minutes (Untimed)	Late adolescents and adults

II. Measures of Specific Job Competencies

Test and Test Type	Description	Time	Target Population
1. Bennett Mechanical Comprehension Test (BMCT) Psychological Corporation [800–211–8378]	Measures understanding of the relationship between physical and mechanical elements	30 minutes (Timed)	Industrial applicants for various mechanical positions
2. Critical Reasoning Test Battery SHL [800–211–8378]	Measures verbal evaluation, data interpretation, and diagrammatic reasoning	80 minutes (Timed)	Supervisors Entry-level managers

Test and Test Type	Description	Time	Target Population
3. Critical Thinking Test (CTT) SHL [800–899–7451]	Measures verbal and numerical reasoning	60 minutes (Timed)	Senior management Middle managers Professionals
4. Differential Aptitude Test (DAT) Psychological Corporation [800–211–8378]	Suite of tests designed to measure ability to learn in nine specific areas	90 minutes (Timed)	Wide range of entry-level job applicants
5. Employee Aptitude Survey (EAS) Psychological Services, Inc. [818–244–0033]	Suite of nine tests designed to measure specific components of mental ability	Eight tests timed at 5 minutes; one at 10	Technical, production, clerical, supervisory, and professional applicants
6. Flanagan Industrial Test (FIT) Pearson Reid/London House [800–221–8378]	Suite of tests designed to measure eighteen different mental abilities	Timing of subtests ranges from 5 to 15 minutes	Lower-level industrial jobs
7. Industrial Reading Test (IRT) Psychological Corporation [800–211–8378]	Measures reading comprehension of technical material	40 minutes (Timed)	Entry-level employment applicants
8. Mathematical Reasoning Test (MRT) HRD Press [800–822–2801]	Assesses mathematical competency up to the college graduate level	30 minutes (Timed)	Middle mgmt. applicants Supervisory applicants
9. Numerical Computational Test HRD Press [800–822–2801]	Designed to measure basic computational skills	15 minutes (Timed)	Supervisory applicants, entry-level office and retail job applicants

Test and Test Type	Description	Time	Target Population
10. Planning, Organizing & Scheduling Test (POST) *HRD Press* [800–822–2801]	Measures planning, organizing, and scheduling of actions and resources in organizations	20 minutes (Timed)	Supervisors, managers, and lower-level executives
11. Sales Ability Test (SAT) *HRD Press* [800–822–2801]	Measures understanding of sales, using sixteen sales scenarios	30 minutes (Untimed)	Entry to mid-level sales jobs
12. Selling Skills Series (SSS) *SHL* [800–899–7451]	Measures facility with written information and the ability to use data	32 minutes	Entry-level retail sales Call-center staff
13. Watson Glaser Critical Thinking Appraisal (WGCT) *Psychological Corporation* [800–211–8378]	Measures ability to think and reason critically and logically	40 minutes (Untimed)	Exempt and non-exempt populations
14. Wide-Range Achievement Test (WRAT-3) *Psychological Corporation* [800–211–8378]	Measures basic reading, spelling, and arithmetic skills	15 to 30 minutes	Entry-level applicants
15. Wonderlic Basic Skills Test (WBST) *Wonderlic Personnel Tests* [800–323–3742]	Designed to measure work-related basic math and verbal skills	40 minutes	Entry-level employment applicants
16. Work Skills Series Production Test (WSSPT) *SHL* [800–899–7451]	Measures basic numerical skills, visual checking, and understanding instructions	Subtests timed from 7 to 12 minutes	Entry-level job applicants for manufacturing and production jobs

III. General Mental Ability Measures

Test and Test Type	Description	Time	Target Population
1. Adaptability Test (AT) *Pearson Reid/London House* [800–221–8378]	Measures verbal, quantitative, and spatial abilities. Yields a single overall score	15 minutes (Timed)	Supervisory, operations, and administrative job applicants.
2. Advanced Mental Abilities Test (AMAT) *HRD Press* [800–822–2801]	Measures general information, vocabulary, logic, and basic arithmetic. Yields a single overall score	25 minutes (Untimed)	Entry-level supervisory, administrative, and craft job applicants
3. Thurstone Test of Mental Alertness (TMA) *Pearson Reid/London House* [800–221–8378]	Measures the ability to learn new skills. Yields scores of quantitative, linguistic, and general mental ability	20 minutes (Timed)	Adolescents and adults
4. Wonderlic Personnel Test (WPT) *Wonderlic Personnel Test* [800–323–3742]	Measures vocabulary, common sense reasoning, arithmetic reasoning, and numerical facility. Yields general mental ability score	12 minutes (Timed)	Adolescents and adults

IV. Miscellaneous Measures
A. Measures of Leadership

Test and Test Type	Description	Time	Target Population
1. Campbell Leadership Index *Reid/London House* [800–221–8378]	Measures twenty-one dimensions of leadership organized in five major orientations	10 to 15 minutes (Untimed)	Adolescents and adults
2. Hogan Development Survey (HDS) *Hogan Assessment Systems* [800–756–0632]	Measures career-derailing tendencies	15 to 20 minutes (Untimed)	Managers and executives, as well as professionals
3. Leadership Opinion Questionnaire (LOQ) *Pearson Reid/London House* [800–221–8378]	Measures the two facets of leadership: consideration and structure	10 minutes (Untimed)	Supervisors and managers
4. Leadership Practices Inventory (LPI) *Jossey-Bass* [877–767–2974]	Measures five practices of "exemplary" leadership	10 to 15 minutes (Untimed)	Supervisors and managers
5. Strategic Leadership Type Indicator *HRD Press* [800–821–2801]	Assesses the leadership style necessary as a function of the level of the subordinate	15 minutes (Untimed)	Supervisors and managers
6. Test of Supervisory Skills (TOSS) *HRD Press* [800–822–2801]	Measures specific skills necessary for supervisory success	15 to 20 minutes (Untimed)	Applicants for supervisory positions
7. Visionary Leader Behavioral Questionnaire (VLBQ) *HRD Press* [800–821–2801]	Measures the behaviors necessary to perform the role of visionary leader	15 to 20 minutes (Untimed)	Supervisors and managers

B. Tests of Integrity/Honesty

Test and Test Type	Description	Time	Target Population
1. Applicant Potential Inventory *Pearson Reid/London House* [800–221–8378]	Provides scores on eight different types of counterproductive behaviors	10 to 15 minutes (Untimed)	Employment applicants
2. CandidCLUES *Psichometrics International, LLC* [888–477–3883]	Provides scores on six different types of counterproductive behavior plus a good impression scale	10 to 15 minutes (Untimed)	Employment applicants
3. Employee Screening Questionnaire (ESQ) *Sigma Assessment Systems* [800–265–1285]	A personality questionnaire; reports five positive and eight counterproductive work behaviors	10 to 15 minutes (Untimed)	Employment applicants
4. Reid Report *Pearson Reid/London House* [800–221–8378]	Reports on four critical behaviors—integrity, anti-social, substance abuse, and job turnover	15 minutes (Untimed)	Employment applicants
5. Stanton Survey *SecurePoint* [888–310–2558]	Measures three counterproductive behaviors: work-related theft, other theft, and violations of company policy	10 to 15 minutes (Untimed)	Employment applicants

References

American Educational Research Association, American Psychological Association, & National Council on Measurement in Education. (1999). *Standards for educational and psychological testing.* Washington, DC: Author.

Barak, A., & English, N. (2002). Prospects and limitations of psychological testing on the internet. *Journal of Technology in Human Services, 19,* 65–89.

Barrick, M.R., & Mount, M.K. (1991). The big five personality dimensions and job performance: A meta-analysis. *Personnel Psychology, 44,* 1–26.

Barrick, M.R., & Mount, M.K. (1993). Autonomy as a moderator of the relationships between the big five personality dimensions and job performance. *Journal of Applied Psychology, 78, 111–118.*

Behling, O. (1998). Employee selection: Will intelligence and conscientiousness do the job? *Academy of Management Executive, 12*(1), 77–86.

Buchanan, T. (2002). On-line assessment: Desirable or dangerous? *Professional Psychology: Research and Practice, 33,* 148–154.

Buchanan, T., Goldberg, L.R., & Johnson, J.A. (1999, November). *WWW personality assessment: Evaluation of an on-line five factor inventory.* Paper presented at the Society for Computers in Psychology, Los Angeles, California.

Butcher, J.N., Perry, J.N., & Atlis, M.M. (2000). Validity and utility of computer-generated test interpretation. *Psychological Assessment, 12,* 6–16.

Camera, W., & Schneider, D.L. (1994). Integrity tests: Facts and unresolved issues. *American Psychologist, 49,* 112–119.

Campbell, K.A., Rohlman, D.S., Storzbach, D., Binder, L.M., Anger, W.K., Kovera, C.A., Davis, K.L., & Grossman, S.J. (1999). Test-retest reliabilities of psychological and neurobehavioral tests self-administered by computer. *Assessment, 6,* 21–32.

Campion, M.A., Palmer, D.K., & Campion, J. (1997). A review of structure in the selection interview. *Personnel Psychology, 50,* 655–702.

Campion, M.A., Pursell, E.D., & Brown, B.K. (1988). Structured interviewing: Raising the psychometric properties of the employment interview. *Personnel Psychology, 41,* 25–42.

Chao, G.T. (1997). Mentoring phases and outcomes. *Journal of Vocational Behavior, 5*, 15–28.

Chao, G.T., Walz, P.M., & Gardner, P.D. (1992). Formal and informal mentorships: A comparison on mentoring functions and contrast with non-mentored counterparts. *Personnel Psychology, 45*, 619–663.

Costa, P.T., Jr., & McCrae, R.R. (1992a). Four ways five factors are basic. *Personality and Individual Differences, 13*, 653–665.

Costa, P.T., Jr., & McCrae, R.R. (1992b). *NEO PI-R professional manual.* Odessa, FL: Psychological Assessment Resources.

Costa, P.T., Jr., & McCrae, R.R. (1992c). *NEO five factor inventory professional manual.* Odessa, FL: Psychological Assessment Resources.

Coynes, I., Warszta, T., & Beadle, S. (2005). The impact of administration on the equivalence of a test battery: A quasi-experimental design. Unpublished manuscript, University of Hull.

Davis, R.N. (1999). Web-based administration of a personality questionnaire: Comparison with traditional methods. *Research Methods, Instruments, & Computers, 31*, 572–577.

Digman, J.M. (1990). Personality structure: Emergence of the five-factor model. In M.R. Rosenzweig & L.W. Porter (Eds.), *Annual Review of Psychology, 41*, 417–440.

DiLalla, D.L. (1996). Computerized administration of the Multidimensional Personality Questionnaire. *Assessment, 3*, 365–374.

Encyclopedia Britannica. (2005). Internet in *Encyclopedia Britannica Almanac 2005.* (CD-ROM version.) Chicago, IL: Author.

Flanagan, J.C. (1954). The critical incident technique. *Psychological Bulletin, 51*, 327–358.

Ghiselli, E.E., Campbell, J.P., & Zedeck, S. (1981). *Measurement theory for the behavioral sciences.* San Francisco: W.H. Freeman.

Goldberg, L.R. (1982a). From ace to zombie: Some explorations in the language of personality. In C.D. Spielberger & J.N. Butcher (Eds.), *Advances in personality assessment* (Vol. 1, pp. 203–234). Hillsdale, NJ: Erlbaum.

Goldberg, L.R. (1982b). The development of markers for the big-five factor structure. *Personality Assessment, 4*, 26–42.

Goldberg, L.R. (1993). The structure of phenotypic personality traits. *American Psychologist, 48*, 26–34.

Goodstein, L.D., & Lanyon, R.I. (1999). Applications of personality assessment to the workplace. *Journal of Business and Psychology, 13*, 291–322.

Hogan, R., & Hogan, J. (1997). *Hogan Development Survey manual.* Tulsa, OK: Hogan Assessment Systems.

Hough, L.M. (1984). Development and evaluation of the "accomplishment record" method of selecting and promoting professions. *Journal of Applied Psychology, 69*, 135–146.

Kram, K.E. (1985). Mentoring at work: Developmental relationships in organizational life. Glenview, IL: Scott Foresman.

Lanyon, R.I., & Goodstein, L.D. (1997). *Psychological assessment* (3rd ed.). New York: John Wiley & Sons.

Latham, G.P., & Saari, L.M. (1984). Do people do what they say? Further studies on the situational interview. *Journal of Applied Psychology, 69,* 569–573.

Matarazzo, J.D. (1990). Psychological assessment versus psychological testing. *American Psychologist, 45,* 999–1017.

McClelland, D.C. (1973). Testing for competence rather than for "intelligence." *American Psychologist, 28,* 1–14.

McCrae, R.R., & Costa, P.T., Jr. (1987). Validation of the five-factor model of personality across instruments and observers. *Journal of Personality and Social Psychology, 52,* 81–90.

McCrae, R.R., & Costa, P.T., Jr. (1990). *Personality and adulthood: Emerging lives, enduring dispositions.* New York: Guilford.

Mead, A.D., & Drasgow, F. (1993). Equivalence of computerized and paper-and-pencil cognitive ability tests: A meta-analysis. *Psychological Bulletin, 114,* 449–458.

Messick, S. (1995). Validity of psychological assessment. *American Psychologist, 50,* 741–749.

Meyer, C.J., Finn, S.F., Eyde, L.D., Kay, G.G., Moreland, K., Dies, R.R., Eisman, E.J., Kubiszyn, T.W., & Reed, G.M. (2001). Psychological testing and psychological assessment: A review of evidence and issues. *American Psychologist, 56,* 128–163.

Naglieri, J.A., Drasgow, F., Schmitt, M., Handler, L., Prifitera, A., Margolis, A., & Velasquez, R. (2004). Psychological testing on the internet: New problems, old issues. *American Psychologist, 59,* 150–162.

Nouman, G., & Baydoun, R. (1998). Computerization of paper-and-pencil tests: When are they equivalent? *Applied Psychological Measurement, 22,* 71–83.

Potosky, D., & Bobko, P. (1997). Computer versus paper-and-pencil administration mode and response distortion in non-cognitive selection tests. *Journal of Applied Psychology, 82,* 293–299.

Prien, E.P., & Goodstein, L.D. (2004). *Test of supervisory skills (TOSS): Test and manual.* Amherst, MA: HRD Press.

Prien, E.P., & Macey, W.H. (1984). Multi-domain job analysis of the industrial-organizational psychologist job. Unpublished manuscript.

Prien, E.P., Schippmann, J.S., & Prien, K.O. (2003). *The practice of individual assessment.* Hillsdale, NJ: Erlbaum.

Primoff, E.S. (1957). The J coefficient approach to jobs and tests. *Personnel Administration, 20,* 77–87.

Reilly, R.R., & Chao, G.T. (1982). Validity and fairness of some alternative employee selection procedures. *Personnel Psychology, 35,* 1–62.

Ryan, A.M., & Sackett, P.R. (1987). A survey of individual assessment practices by I/O psychologists. *Personnel Psychology, 40,* 455–488.

Schippmann, J.S., Hawthorne, S.L., & Schmidt, S.D. (1992). Work roles and training needs for the practice of industrial and organizational psychology at the master's and Ph.D. level. *Journal of Business and Psychology, 6,* 325–354.

Schippmann, J.S., & Prien, E.P. (1989). An assessment of the contributions of general mental ability and personality characteristics to managerial success. *Journal of Business and Psychology, 3,* 423–437.

Schippmann, J.S., Prien, E.P., & Katz, J.A. (1990). Reliability and validity of in-basket performance measures. *Personnel Psychology, 43,* 1–17.

Schmidt, F.L. (2002). The role of general cognitive ability and job performance: Why there cannot be a debate. *Human Performance, 15,* 187–211.

Schmidt, F.L., & Hunter, J.E. (1998). The validity and utility of selection methods in personnel psychology: Practical and theoretical implications of 85 years of research findings. *Psychological Bulletin, 124,* 262–274.

Schmidt, F.L., Hunter, J.E., Croll, P.R., & McKenzie, R.C. (1983). Estimation of employment test validities by expert judgment. *Journal of Applied Psychology, 68,* 590–601.

Society for Industrial and Organizational Psychology, Inc. (2003). *Principles for the validation and use of personnel selection procedures* (4th ed.). Bowling Green, OH: Author.

Tett, R.P., Jackson, D.N., & Rothstein, M. (1991). Personality measures as predictors of job performance. *Personnel Psychology, 44,* 703–742.

Uniform Guidelines on Employee Selection Procedures. 43 Fed. Reg. 38295–38309 (1978).

Van de Vijer, H., Fons, J.R., & Harsfeldt, M. (1994). The incomplete equivalence of the paper-and-pencil and computerized versions of the General Aptitude Battery. *Journal of Applied Psychology, 79,* 852–859.

Wallace, P. (1999). *The psychology of the internet.* Cambridge, UK: Cambridge University Press.

About the Authors

Leonard D. Goodstein, Ph.D., a consulting psychologist based in Washington, D.C., specializes in providing consultation in personality assessment, especially in the workplace—as well as executive development, including executive coaching. He is also a Principal with Professional Assessment Services and Solutions (PASS), Psichometrics International, LLC, and Forensic Sciences Medical Group, PC.

After receiving his bachelor's degree with honors from the City College of New York, Dr. Goodstein went on to receive both an M.A. and Ph.D. from Columbia University, both in psychology. A holder of the Diploma in Clinical Psychology of the American Board of Professional Psychology, Dr. Goodstein is a Distinguished Practitioner of the National Academy of Practice. He is a licensed psychologist in both California and the District of Columbia. Dr. Goodstein is listed in *Who's Who in America* and *American Men and Women in Science*.

Since completing a three-year term as executive vice president and chief executive officer of the American Psychological Association, psychology's national membership association, in 1988 he has been engaged in consulting, research, and writing. Prior to APA, Dr. Goodstein had a distinguished academic career, including professorships at the Universities of Iowa, Cincinnati, and Arizona State, where he served as chair of the Department of Psychology. In addition, he has been a Fulbright Senior Lecturer (Professor) at the Vrije Universiteit in the Netherlands. After leaving academia and prior to joining APA, he was president and later chairman of the board of University Associates, Inc., now Pfeiffer.

Erich P. Prien, Ph.D., an industrial/organizational psychologist based in Memphis, Tennessee, specializes in the development, standardization, and application of psychological tests, especially in the workplace. He is also the founder and president of Performance Management Press (PMP), which has been the principal marketing arm for his tests.

Following receipt of his bachelor's degree from Western Michigan University, he received an MA from Carnegie Mellon University and a Ph.D. from Western Reserve University (now Case Western Reserve), both in industrial/organizational psychology. Dr. Prien has served as a research psychologist for the Standard Oil Company, as assistant director of the Psychological Research Service at Case Western University, as adviser to the Imperial Iranian Armed Forces, and as a faculty member at Greensboro College, University of Akron, Georgia Technical University, and the University of Memphis. After leaving the University of Memphis in 1987, Dr. Prien has devoted himself to his professional practice, his research, and his sustained interest in writing.

Dr. Prien is a fellow of the American Psychological Association and the Society for Industrial and Organizational Psychology and holds the Diploma in Industrial Psychology from the American Board of Professional Psychology. Among his many awards are the Distinguished Professional Award from the Society for Industrial and Organizational Psychology, the Author of the Year Award from The American Society of Training Directors and the *Journal of Performance and Instruction*, and he was the Creativity Research Award Winner from the American Society for Personnel Administration twice.

Index

A

ACT (American College Test), 23
Administrative/professional job assessment, 74*e*
Agreeableness, 44
American Educational Research Association, 5
American Psychological Association, 5, 26
American Society for Training and Development, 11
Analytical/technical job assessment, 75*e*
Anger, W. K., 25
Assessors: additional considerations/recommendations for, 14–15; final report made by, 108–125; individual assessment report responsibilities of, 19, 22; as instrument of assessment and prediction, 42; psychological measurements and role of, 42–43; three levels of competencies for, 9–14; what they need to know, 8–9. *See also* Final report; Human resources (HR); Individual assessment
Atlis, M. M., 28

B

Barak, A., 28
Barrick, M. R., 44
Basic clerical/office job assessment, 74*e*
Baydoun, R., 25
Beadle, S., 25
Behavior: data from observed, 95–96; HDS scales on counterproductive, 129–131; problem of counterproductive, 50; team building, 132–134; tests for predicting intelligent, 40; tests for predicting work, 44–46. *See also* Psychological tests
Behling, O., 49
Benchmarking: additional reasons for, 81–82; advantages of using, 78–79; case example of, 81; concurrent validity established by, 39, 82; conducting, 79–81; definition of, 78; limitations of, 82; validity established by, 39
"Big Five" prediction factors, 44–45
Binder, L. M., 25
BMI (Body Mass Index), 31

Pfeiffer Publications Guide

This guide is designed to familiarize you with the various types of Pfeiffer publications. The formats section describes the various types of products that we publish; the methodologies section describes the many different ways that content might be provided within a product. We also provide a list of the topic areas in which we publish.

FORMATS

In addition to its extensive book-publishing program, Pfeiffer offers content in an array of formats, from fieldbooks for the practitioner to complete, ready-to-use training packages that support group learning.

FIELDBOOK Designed to provide information and guidance to practitioners in the midst of action. Most fieldbooks are companions to another, sometimes earlier, work, from which its ideas are derived; the fieldbook makes practical what was theoretical in the original text. Fieldbooks can certainly be read from cover to cover. More likely, though, you'll find yourself bouncing around following a particular theme, or dipping in as the mood, and the situation, dictate.

HANDBOOK A contributed volume of work on a single topic, comprising an eclectic mix of ideas, case studies, and best practices sourced by practitioners and experts in the field.

An editor or team of editors usually is appointed to seek out contributors and to evaluate content for relevance to the topic. Think of a handbook not as a ready-to-eat meal, but as a cookbook of ingredients that enables you to create the most fitting experience for the occasion.

RESOURCE Materials designed to support group learning. They come in many forms: a complete, ready-to-use exercise (such as a game); a comprehensive resource on one topic (such as conflict management) containing a variety of methods and approaches; or a collection of like-minded activities (such as icebreakers) on multiple subjects and situations.

TRAINING PACKAGE An entire, ready-to-use learning program that focuses on a particular topic or skill. All packages comprise a guide for the facilitator/trainer and a workbook for the participants. Some packages are supported with additional media—such as video—or learning aids, instruments, or other devices to help participants understand concepts or practice and develop skills.

- *Facilitator/trainer's guide* Contains an introduction to the program, advice on how to organize and facilitate the learning event, and step-by-step instructor notes. The guide also contains copies of presentation materials—handouts, presentations, and overhead designs, for example—used in the program.

- *Participant's workbook* Contains exercises and reading materials that support the learning goal and serves as a valuable reference and support guide for participants in the weeks and months that follow the learning event. Typically, each participant will require his or her own workbook.

ELECTRONIC CD-ROMs and web-based products transform static Pfeiffer content into dynamic, interactive experiences. Designed to take advantage of the searchability, automation, and ease-of-use that technology provides, our e-products bring convenience and immediate accessibility to your workspace.

METHODOLOGIES

CASE STUDY A presentation, in narrative form, of an actual event that has occurred inside an organization. Case studies are not prescriptive, nor are they used to prove a point; they are designed to develop critical analysis and decision-making skills. A case study has a specific time frame, specifies a sequence of events, is narrative in structure, and contains a plot structure—an issue (what should be/have been done?). Use case studies when the goal is to enable participants to apply previously learned theories to the circumstances in the case, decide what is pertinent, identify the real issues, decide what should have been done, and develop a plan of action.

ENERGIZER A short activity that develops readiness for the next session or learning event. Energizers are most commonly used after a break or lunch to stimulate or refocus the group. Many involve some form of physical activity, so they are a useful way to counter post-lunch lethargy. Other uses include transitioning from one topic to another, where "mental" distancing is important.

EXPERIENTIAL LEARNING ACTIVITY (ELA) A facilitator-led intervention that moves participants through the learning cycle from experience to application (also known as a Structured Experience). ELAs are carefully thought-out designs in which there is a definite learning purpose and intended outcome. Each step—everything that participants do during the activity—facilitates the accomplishment of the stated goal. Each ELA includes complete instructions for facilitating the intervention and a clear statement of goals, suggested group size and timing, materials required, an explanation of the process, and, where appropriate, possible variations to the activity. (For more detail on Experiential Learning Activities, see the Introduction to the *Reference Guide to Handbooks and Annuals*, 1999 edition, Pfeiffer, San Francisco.)

GAME A group activity that has the purpose of fostering team spirit and togetherness in addition to the achievement of a pre-stated goal. Usually contrived—undertaking a desert expedition, for example—this type of learning method offers an engaging means for participants to demonstrate and practice business and interpersonal skills. Games are effective for team building and personal development mainly because the goal is subordinate to the process—the means through which participants reach decisions, collaborate, communicate, and generate trust and understanding. Games often engage teams in "friendly" competition.

ICEBREAKER A (usually) short activity designed to help participants overcome initial anxiety in a training session and/or to acquaint the participants with one another. An icebreaker can be a fun activity or can be tied to specific topics or training goals. While a useful tool in itself, the icebreaker comes into its own in situations where tension or resistance exists within a group.

INSTRUMENT A device used to assess, appraise, evaluate, describe, classify, and summarize various aspects of human behavior. The term used to describe an instrument depends primarily on its format and purpose. These terms include survey, questionnaire, inventory, diagnostic, survey, and poll. Some uses of instruments include providing instrumental feedback to group members, studying here-and-now processes or functioning within a group, manipulating group composition, and evaluating outcomes of training and other interventions.

Instruments are popular in the training and HR field because, in general, more growth can occur if an individual is provided with a method for focusing specifically on his or her own behavior. Instruments also are used to obtain information that will serve as a basis for change and to assist in workforce planning efforts.

Paper-and-pencil tests still dominate the instrument landscape with a typical package comprising a facilitator's guide, which offers advice on administering the instrument and interpreting the collected data, and an initial set of instruments. Additional instruments are available separately. Pfeiffer, though, is investing heavily in e-instruments. Electronic instrumentation provides effortless distribution and, for larger groups particularly, offers advantages over paper-and-pencil tests in the time it takes to analyze data and provide feedback.

LECTURETTE A short talk that provides an explanation of a principle, model, or process that is pertinent to the participants' current learning needs. A lecturette is intended to establish a common language bond between the trainer and the participants by providing a mutual frame of reference. Use a lecturette as an introduction to a group activity or event, as an interjection during an event, or as a handout.

MODEL A graphic depiction of a system or process and the relationship among its elements. Models provide a frame of reference and something more tangible, and more easily remembered, than a verbal explanation. They also give participants something to "go on," enabling them to track their own progress as they experience the dynamics, processes, and relationships being depicted in the model.

ROLE PLAY A technique in which people assume a role in a situation/ scenario: a customer service rep in an angry-customer exchange, for example. The way in which the role is approached is then discussed and feedback is offered. The role play is often repeated using a different approach and/or incorporating changes made based on feedback received. In other words, role playing is a spontaneous interaction involving realistic behavior under artificial (and safe) conditions.

SIMULATION A methodology for understanding the interrelationships among components of a system or process. Simulations differ from games in that they test or use a model that depicts or mirrors some aspect of reality in form, if not necessarily in content. Learning occurs by studying the effects of change on one or more factors of the model. Simulations are commonly used to test hypotheses about what happens in a system—often referred to as "what if?" analysis—or to examine best-case/worst-case scenarios.

THEORY A presentation of an idea from a conjectural perspective. Theories are useful because they encourage us to examine behavior and phenomena through a different lens.

TOPICS

The twin goals of providing effective and practical solutions for workforce training and organization development and meeting the educational needs of training and human resource professionals shape Pfeiffer's publishing program. Core topics include the following:

Leadership & Management

Communication & Presentation

Coaching & Mentoring

Training & Development

e-Learning

Teams & Collaboration

OD & Strategic Planning

Human Resources

Consulting

What will you find on pfeiffer.com?

- The best in workplace performance solutions for training and HR professionals

- Downloadable training tools, exercises, and content

- Web-exclusive offers

- Training tips, articles, and news

- Seamless online ordering

- Author guidelines, information on becoming a Pfeiffer Affiliate, and much more

Discover more at www.pfeiffer.com